William Ramage Lawson

Spain of today: a descriptive, industrial, and financial survey of the

peninsula

With a full account of the Rio Tinto mines

William Ramage Lawson

Spain of today: a descriptive, industrial, and financial survey of the peninsula
With a full account of the Rio Tinto mines

ISBN/EAN: 9783337229610

Printed in Europe, USA, Canada, Australia, Japan

Cover: Foto ©Andreas Hilbeck / pixelio.de

More available books at **www.hansebooks.com**

·SPAIN OF TO-DAY·

A DESCRIPTIVE, INDUSTRIAL, AND FINANCIAL
SURVEY OF THE PENINSULA

*WITH A FULL ACCOUNT OF THE
RIO TINTO MINES*

BY

W. R. LAWSON

WILLIAM BLACKWOOD AND SONS
EDINBURGH AND LONDON
MDCCCXC

CONTENTS.

Contents.

SPAIN OF TO-DAY.

CROSSING THE PYRENEES.

IN spite of Sydney Smith's warning, people have
been tempted to speak disrespectfully of the equa-
tor, but I never heard of any one being so far left
to himself as to speak disrespectfully of the Pyrenees.   They are one of the few geographical institutions of Europe which maintain the freshness of
their reputation and the dignity of their traditions.
More fortunate than the Alps, they have not had
their veil of mystery torn aside, and a horde of
Cook's tourists let loose on them, armed with
Baedekers and hotel coupons.   A sympathetic pilgrim may still wander about in the villages of the
Pyrenees and feast his soul on the grandest soli-
tudes as well as the most enchanting beauties.
Show places like Biarritz and Arcachon are mere
pin-points in a world of loveliness all its own.
They are but fringes on which fashion has capri-

A

ciously settled, leaving the main body of the great
mountain-chain untouched.

Where the Pyrenees begin and where they end I
do not profess to know, for this time I have purposely avoided guide-books. Three days of continual railway travelling among them has left
my mind filled with a jumble of vivid pictures—
gigantic ribs of primeval rock standing out wild
and desolate against the horizon ; valleys in endless
variety winding in and out between the mountains,
sometimes a broad expanse of meadows and wheat
fields, sometimes a narrow gorge black with live
oaks ; yellow muddy torrents roaring down the
mountain - side, or sweeping along in a resistless
current below; now and then glimpses of sea-
coast breaking in suddenly and changing the
whole face of the scene. That is the special
charm of the Pyrenees, distinguishing it above
every rival in the Old World or the New. It wants
nothing essential to magnificent scenery. Land
and sea, mountain and valley, stream and forest,
are all blended in one noble harmony.

Elsewhere there may be finer individual sights.
The snow - capped Mont Blanc and Pilatus are
wanting, but they have no Atlantic Ocean dashing
itself against their feet. The largest and deepest
of the Pyrenean valleys would be lost a hundred
times over in the terrific depth and breadth of
the 2000 feet ravine which the Mexican Railway hangs over like a thread of gossamer, but it
has the drawback that it flashes on the spectator

in a moment, and the first flash stuns him. His mind is overwhelmed, and he can take in no stronger impression. The Pyrenees do not surprise him with these electric shocks. Their grandeur, impressive as it often is, is never blinding, but unfolds itself gently to the eye, and grows as it is lingered on. Often it sinks into mere prettiness, like that of a Warwickshire or a Surrey landscape. Then the turn of a corner or a rush through a tunnel will conjure up some wilder vision than ever. Faster than the eye can follow, the wide-reaching panorama is continually changing, both in mood and form. Its smiles and its frowns merge rapidly into each other, until the traveller has to resign himself meekly to the thought that he has dropped into an enchanted kaleidoscope.

In coming from Paris the Pyrenees begin, I presume, at Bayonne. For miles before that, however, the country is hilly, though not mountainous. Even on the north side of Bordeaux the railway has a stiff climb occasionally, and from Bordeaux onward the scenery is distinctively highland. The air has a sharp, bracing scent, and a fine panorama of hills stretches on either side. Down to Bayonne is a gradual descent till we reach the broad marshes which encircle the chief port of the Pyrenees. Now the ascent begins again in earnest, and the train has a stiff pull up to Biarritz, the road being a succession of tunnels and inclines. The once-famous but now decaying Capua of the Second Empire makes very little show from the railway.

The station itself is still smart and well kept, and in the distance it has a background of handsome villas peeping out from the pine-woods; but Biarritz proper is not visible, and is hardly worth a day's labour to hunt up. Just beyond it there are prettier gems of natural beauty.

The next station to Biarritz—Guethary—has of late become a strong rival to it. After twenty minutes of panting up hills and rushing through dark tunnels, the train all at once shoots out on a shelf of rock, at the foot of which the Atlantic breakers are rolling in with a heavy boom. Two minutes' walk from the station takes you down to the beach. The bay is quite narrow—merely a little corner of the Bay of Biscay that has cut a sharp dent into the mountain-barrier which holds back the Bay itself. Immediately beyond the sea is lost again, and does not reappear till St Jean de Luz, which, though a much more important place than our little Guethary, is not to be compared with it in picturesqueness. Guethary consists as yet of only about a dozen houses perched on the cliffs; two or three of them are hotels and the rest villas. But it is becoming popular as a bathing-place, and its season, from July to September, is every year more prosperous. Parties making a round of the Pyrenees are also beginning to take a few weeks of it on their way to Arcachon.

St Jean de Luz, Hendaye, and other frontier towns, which used to be strongholds of the Carlists, seem now to have retired from the revolutionary

business. They have turned over a new leaf, and
find it much more profitable to cultivate lumber
than politics. An enormous lumber trade is growing upon the French side of the Pyrenees, where
the facilities for shipment at Hendaye and Bayonne are extensive. Every station has its timber-
yard, covered with high piles of rough-cut boards,
from which waggons are being loaded all day long.
From Hendaye onward the coast becomes more
deeply indented. Broad stretches of flat land
intrude themselves between the mountains, and
some of them end in valleys running far up into
the interior. They bring down considerable streams
of water, which at their mouth are navigable for
small craft, and with a moderate outlay might be
made the groundwork of good harbours. In that
respect the country has infinite capabilities which
have hardly been touched yet. Where now one
sees a small coaster in mid-stream, there might be
forests of shipping all profitably employed.

Irun, the first station on the Spanish frontier,
stands on one of the flats into which the coast dips
every now and then. Here the Pyrenees take a
fresh start and begin to rise steadily. San Sebastian, about eleven miles further on, is now a
flourishing port, having completely recovered from
the sad knocking about it got in the Carlist war.
The railway now quits the coast, and has to attack
the centre of the range, scaling steep mountain-
slopes, cutting for itself narrow ledges along the
face of sheer precipices, and, as a last resort, tun-

nelling a way through where climbing becomes impossible. The Great Northern of Spain, which has had all these engineering feats to accomplish, is one of the most remarkable railways on the Continent, and having got well over the difficulties of its youth, it is now entering on a harvest of prosperity.

SPANISH PILGRIMS.

THE absent, we are told, are always in the wrong, and Spain is in that category as a nation. To the rest of Europe it is very much absent, and in reputation it suffers accordingly. When I confidentially intimated to a friend or two that Spain might be worth looking up, one and all of them tried to dissuade me from it as a waste of time. There was nothing to see in the Peninsula, they said, but beggars and bad cooking. "And the people are so awfully behind the age! It would be like sliding back a century or two to go near them." Nevertheless, I have taken the risk of spending a hot month in Spain, and of seeing the country from end to end. There is a Spanish proverb— not a very old one, and I should not wonder if some sceptical readers were to blame me for it— that to get through the work properly there will have to be three resurrection days : one for the world at large ; a second, five hundred years later, for Spain ; and the third, another five hundred

years later, for the Spanish railways. It is to be
hoped that the Spanish railways will be ready,
even then.   But, to be just to them, they are
waking up, and, if not marvels of rapidity, they
have other virtues quite as important. Sir Edward
Watkin may be surprised to hear that they are
exceedingly punctual. I have not found a train
yet behind time; but then it would tax all the
ingenuity of guards and engine-drivers not to keep
ahead of a time-table which seems to have been
originally based on the travelling powers of a mule
team. What needs waking up is the time-table
itself, which might have been framed by Noah as
marching orders for the animals leaving the ark.
Old George Stephenson would have thought it a
trifle slow between Stockton and Darlington sixty
years ago.

But, such as it is, the Spaniards faithfully adhere
to it. They are by nature a punctual, orderly
people. The mischief with them is, not that they
fall behind time, for their trains seldom do that; it
is that they lay out their time as if they had all
eternity to draw on. If they made up their minds
to run their trains thirty kilomètres an hour instead
of about twenty kilomètres an hour, doubtless they
would conscientiously live up to their new rule.
Already the South Express, running twice a-week
from Paris to Madrid and Lisbon, has made a considerable difference, having cut down the running
time on the Spanish section of the route by seven
or eight hours. On the other hand, there is a good

deal to say for the Spanish system. It is well to have one country left in Europe which keeps itself out of the hurly-burly, where the graces of dignity and deliberation are still practised, and lazy men can count on a congenial refuge. For a constitutionally busy man it is like a soothing medicine merely to loaf about in Spain with his hands in his pockets. He need not speak to anybody or trouble his head about anything, but simply look on. It would calm the most fevered soul to witness the starting of a Spanish train, especially if it happens to be called an express. Even the perturbed spirit of Hamlet's father might, after such a scene, have returned to its sulphurous fires with greater resignation. As for me, I have repeatedly found it the best possible sort of a siesta.

Par example: You arrive at a junction, say about mid-day, and have to change trains. Provision has been thoughtfully made for giving you time to eat two lunches if you feel inclined, to spend a sweet half-hour over your cigar and coffee, then to promenade for another half-hour in the pleasant company of a second manilla. Now you may, without risk of being suspected of impatience, begin to ask for your train. It will be pointed out to you in three or four sections, standing about in the yard, with a few other trains in the same fragmentary stage. The engine, snorting and shrieking in the distance—Spanish engines can shriek well, if they do nothing else—is probably making them up. A quarter of an hour later you may venture to put another question, and this time your train will be coming alongside the platform.

Then the general leave-taking begins—a very interesting and affecting ceremony in Spanish railway life. There is none of your dog-in-the-manger exclusiveness about a Spanish railway platform. It is like original sin and the hooping-cough—open to all. If a son or a daughter be leaving home on a dreadful journey of ten miles or so, the whole family will come down to mingle tears and kisses till the last moment. The father will be there in his best mosaic pants—blue and red for choice; and the mother in her excitement will have forgotten her mantilla and rushed forth in a plain cotton gown. Perhaps the dear old grandmother has been able to come down with them, and she stands a little in the rear, with a dry smile on her puckered face, and ready to strike in with a blessing at the finish. But when there is much kissing to do she may have to wait a pretty long while for her turn. Kisses are given and received in duplicate, one on each cheek, with sometimes an extra one on the forehead for luck.

The farewell music is in a different key when one of the señoritas of the village starts on a railway journey. She descends on the railway station with an escort of all the young Lochinvars for miles round. They get her ticket for her, hand her into the carriage, and get in beside her by relays of half a dozen each to entertain her during the last ten minutes, which often stretch out for a full hour.

While the poet of the party pays her compliments which might have fallen from the lips of Cervantes, the guitar-man reels off her favourite air, and the generally - useful man runs to the *cantena* for a glass of iced lemonade. Statistics prove that the lemonade man invariably gets her in the end. Your Spanish maiden is becoming practical, like most other maidens nowadays. She reasons with herself that poetry and music may be nice to sweeten life with, but are rather thin to live on.

While the *addios* are at their hottest, the guards, porters, and other official hangers - round look on with approving sympathy. They have no thought to spare for anything else, nor have the waiters in the *fonda*, or buffet, who steal out with their napkins over their arms, and pretend to be serving imaginary customers in the train, though every eye in their heads declares that they too are Lochinvars at heart. Suddenly the tinkle of a bell is heard. Anywhere else it would be a note of alarm. As the nigger observed when he was asked to say something about hen-stealing in his revival sermon, "it would cast a chill on the meeting." But in Spain train bells have long ceased to be formidable. Familiarity with them has bred con-tempt, and little attention is paid even to the third or fourth ringing. The first bell is popularly understood to signify that the porters must leave off flirting and borrowing cigars from the passen-gers; the second is a hint to the engine-driver to finish his lunch, and at the third the guards begin to slam the carriage doors recklessly as a warning to stragglers to get aboard. Ten minutes or a quarter of an hour afterwards the head guard takes out his pocket bagpipes and gives a groan on them suggestive of a whole cart-load of pigs being suddenly squashed. Then he means business, and five minutes later the engine responds with a shriek almost as blood-curdling. It signifies, I believe, that excuses for delay are exhausted, and no more fun is to be got at that station till next time.

BILBAO AND ITS IRON MINES.

SPAIN is not only a richly endowed country, but it has an unusual share of special endowments. There is but one Rio Tinto in the world; the quicksilver mines of Almaden are almost equally unique, and Europe has nothing to compare either in magnitude or value with the hematite iron deposits of Bilbao. It has become a fashion of late, especially among promoters of rival iron mines, to speak of Bilbao as being on the wane. The hematite beds or quarries are, it is said, shallow, and already show signs of giving out. Official statistics do not, however, offer much countenance to that theory. They fluctuate, it is true, very erratically from year to year, but that is rather owing to variations of demand than of supply. Spanish hematite goes all over the world and has many different markets to depend on. Their requirements are not always uniform. Some of them may, owing to special causes, double their consumption, while others almost cease to be consumers. The United States is a peculiarly capricious customer. Last year (1888) its imports from Bilbao fell away nearly to nothing, but just now, I believe, it is making up for it. Since 1883 the total exports of ore from Bilbao have exceeded three million tons per annum. In 1887 they exceeded four million tons, and 1889 will show perhaps half a million tons increase on that. Acting-Consul Larrea reports the actual totals of the past quinquennium as follows :—

	TONS.
1884	3,370,000
1885	3,155,000
1886	3,295,000
1887	4,170,000
1888	3,591,000

The decline in 1888 was partly nominal and partly due to exceptional causes. Small ports outside of Bilbao bar are now getting part of the shipping trade. In 1888 they exported over 320,000 tons, besides which nearly 40,000 were sent coastwise. With these additions, the apparently reduced total of 1888 comes very close to that of 1887. When we bring into account the pig-iron exports the balance turns the other way. Since the shipping facilities of the port were fully developed, English coal can be laid down so cheaply that it pays to smelt on the spot. The local smelting-works are increasing both in number and size, and in future the proportion of hematite shipped in the form of pig-iron will steadily go on at the expense of ore shipments. Last year (1888) it amounted to fully 135,000 tons, of which the largest portion went to Italy (58,755 tons), and the next largest (48,888 tons) to other Spanish ports. These two markets absorbed more than four-fifths of the entire export, leaving less than 30,000 tons for elsewhere. Holland took 9200 tons; Germany, 8780 tons; France, 5270 tons; Portugal, 1900 tons, and Russia 1350 tons. The other consignments were all under 1000 tons, the smallest having been our own — an evidently experimental lot of 100 tons, sent by the Altos Hornos Company to England.

Biscaya, of which Bilbao is the capital, is altogether a peculiar and highly privileged corner of Spain. It seems to have everything that a community can wish for, whether in political distinction or commercial prosperity. For its gallant resistance to the Carlists, when they laid siege to it instead of boldly marching to Madrid, as they should have done, Bilbao is for all time coming entitled to style itself *la Invicta*. More substantial honours than that have also been showered on it by the Government. In 1887 it was visited by the Queen Regent, who became enthusiastic in her admiration of its busy quays, its beautiful river Nervion, lined with ships of all nations, its gay streets, and its un-Spanish air of activity. Her Majesty was won over at once to the ambitious scheme of an outer harbour, which was the burning question of the day among the Bilbaons. The scheme was there and then formally sanctioned,

and its execution is now making rapid and visible
progress. Part of the design is to make Bilbao
a great arsenal and naval yard, for which it has
undeniable advantages. By way of a start the
Spanish Government gave it a commission for five
ironclads—an order large enough to have caused
some excitement even on the Clyde.

Since the Queen Regent's visit things have gone
well with Bilbao, and little wonder that it should
be the most loyal of Spanish cities, both to the
Queen herself and to the throne of which she has
been so opportune and so irresistible a defender.
In this respect, Bilbao on the Atlantic side of the
Peninsula and Barcelona on the Mediterranean
side are the antipodes of each other—the one a hot-
bed of republicanism, and the other a bulwark of
conservatism and loyalty. Both prosper, though
in different ways ; both are powerful in a different
spirit. Only a loose-jointed, inchoate country like
Spain could hold together two such opposites as
these chief cities of the Biscayans and the Catalans.
The conservatism of the Biscayans is largely tem-
pered by foreign blood and enterprise. Bilbao
itself is almost entirely the creation of British
and German capital. The mineral wealth of the
Somorrostro mountains has been known from time
immemorial; and it could not well fail to be, for the
richest iron-ore stares you in the face out of steep
banks many hundred feet high. The Goldames
mine is a huge cliff, about a mile long and 280 feet
in height, composed of solid hematite, which can

be cut out like stone or marble. It is run right through the hill by a tunnel nearly a quarter of a mile long, down to the river-side at Portugalete, where it is tipped into the ship's hold with the same ease as Rio Tinto ore at Huelva.

Like Lady Jane in "Patience," the Somorrostro iron deposits are distinguished by their massiveness. They form huge basins or quarries in the primeval beds of limestone. Some of them are worked as "open casts," after the manner of the chief deposit in Rio Tinto. Others need only to be quarried out of the face of the hill. Their situation has done as much for them as their size and quality. Lying within a radius of ten or twelve miles from tide water, they have lent themselves readily to the cheapest possible forms of transport. Wire tramways connect the principal mines with wharves of their own, which steamers can lie alongside of and receive cargo as fast as it can be tumbled into them. Surface railways are also largely in use. In the lower parts of Bilbao the river-side is gridironed with iron rails running in from the mines. Five of these are independent undertakings, all doing well. The Triano line carries a third of all the ore shipped from the port; the Orcanero claims a fourth, and the Bilbao river a fifth. There are besides two small lines, the Franco-Belge and the Regato, which are gradually struggling into a good traffic.

Hematite is king in Bilbao and all round about it. Practically, the same men own the mines, the railways, the local banks, and the best part of the town itself. Like the distillers of Campbeltown, whose motto is " Whisky first, last, and all the time," they know only one form of wealth, and it is iron. Three-fourths of the money they take out of their mines or blast-furnaces goes back into them again. They have no notion of any other speculation or investment. As their money accumulates they keep it in the bank until a good opportunity occurs to reconvert it into hematite.

For a Spanish town Bilbao is not merely well-to-do, but it has a wonderful command of hard cash. Communities so situated generally mortgage their future very freely, and keep little of their wealth in a liquid form, but Bilbao has always a handsome balance at its bankers. Acting - Consul Larrea mentions as a remarkable illustration of this that the Bank of Bilbao, according to its last issued report, had on deposit, not bearing interest, the enormous sum of *ten millions sterling !* I doubt if there be in all Europe another town of 40,000 souls which can say ditto to that, or even get half-way towards it. An English provincial town with a population of 40,000 would be apt to crow if it could show a single million of deposits, savings banks included.

A TABLE D'HÔTE AT BURGOS.

WHEN you are at Burgos, of course you will go to the cathedral. 'Murray's Handbook' will see that you do your duty there. It will tell you what to admire in the stonework, in the huge gilded altars, in the rare Murillos, and the still rarer tapestries, of which Burgos cathedral has the finest collection existing in the world. A wide corridor enclosing one of the many chapels is hung all round on both sides with broad tapestry curtains, any one of which would cause a sensation at Christie & Manson's. The whole history of Spain is told in them by deft fingers long dead and forgotten. Adam and Eve are there still happy in the Garden of Eden; the Apostles in bright green cloaks are hauling in fish in red nets; Charles the Fifth has no thought as yet of retiring to his monastery; and Philip the Second is surrounded by his heretic-burning doctors of the Holy Inquisition.

Admire all the tapestries, listen for a few minutes

to the beautiful singing of the choir, which seems
to go on from morning to night, and then wander
out into the neighbouring *plaza* to consider what
you will do next. You feel disposed, perhaps, to
dine, and you would naturally prefer a real Spanish
dinner if you can get one. But how to get it is
the question. There are no hotels visible. Burgos
is a large city, and evidently prosperous. Its
streets, though narrow, are clean and well paved.
It has a fine public garden running alongside of
a bright sparkling river, crossed at intervals by
picturesque bridges. By the side of the *Almaden*
a fair is going on, and show-booths, gypsies, organ-
grinders, are all doing good business. There are
even phrenologists, chiropodists, and penny balloon
men, exactly as at Yarmouth. The only old friend
you will miss is the Salvation Army. It has not
yet got so far south as this charming sleepy
Burgos. But one cannot dine very well at a
Spanish fair. He may get roasted chestnuts off a
charcoal brazier, or *tortillas* swimming in oil; but
these, though unquestionably dishes of the country,
are not, as Mrs Grundy would say, very satisfying.

You wander along the *Almaden* looking for a
hotel, and wondering how the hotel - keepers of
Burgos ever expect to find guests if they keep so
carefully out of the way. *Cafés* enough there are,
all full of little tables, at which the soothing coffee
and the stimulating cognac are being dispensed,
but there is no sign of eating. It is useless to
consult the marble statue of a royal Philip or

Ferdinand, who stands with his back to the river and his face looking towards the *plaza*. He may have been a *gourmet* in his day, but he is done with it all now. If you make bold to stop a man in uniform, under the impression that he is a policeman, he may be the *Alcalde* himself, or an *Extremo Excellenso* of the municipal council. Hotels are probably not much in his line either. He is familiar with *posadas*, and has observed that when a *posada* or tavern grows ambitious it calls itself a *fonda;* but the provincial Spaniard travels seldom, and does very little public eating. His festive evenings are spent at the theatre, or in solemnly driving up and down the *Almaden*, under the shade of the chestnut-trees. It is not for him that hotels are needed, and he cares very little whether they be on the *plaza* or in the narrowest, darkest back street of Burgos.

True, you might long ago have got out of your fix by consulting Murray. He would very probably have recommended you to go to the *Fonda del Norte*, which, however, would not have brought you much further on your way. If the *Fonda del Norte* be the chief hotel in Burgos, it should not be very difficult to find ; but, like Noah's dove, you have wandered up and down all the *calles* and *puertes* in Burgos seeking rest for the sole of your foot and finding none. You may have minutely inspected every building in the place without discovering a signboard, or a brass-plate, or a porter's cap with a gold band, or any other symbol whatever of lodging

for man and beast. Once you may have strayed
into a broad, gloomy hall, hoping it might be the
outworks of a *fonda*, but only to learn from the
Gorgon at the rear that it is a seminary for girls.
Another time a broad paved corridor may have
tempted you in, only to learn that the local
receiver of taxes had got you in his toils. All
the while your appetite sharpens, and the question
where they keep their hotels in Burgos becomes,
as the Spaniards say, more " palpitating."

At last, when you are about to give up the
search, you pass a wide-open door, at the mouth of
which is an odd-looking vehicle, a cross between a
diligence and an omnibus. Painted on the back of
it is the legend *Fonda del Norte.* By the side of
the big door is a little one leading into a dark
recess, larger than a sentry-box, but hardly big
enough to be called a room. It is the front office
of the *Fonda del Norte*, modestly furnished with a
decrepit desk and two or three benches, originally
covered with leather, but now quite indifferent to
appearances. On the wall hangs a yellow placard,
which you have already seen and studied in many
a railway waiting-room on your way down. It is
the time-table of the Northern Railway of Spain
for the year 1883, I think, or it might have been
1885. A couple of years, however, is of no consequence in Spanish railway chronology. Railway
managers would as soon think of taking up the
rails as of changing the trains. Before leaving
London a friend gave me an old Spanish Bradshaw

of the year 1885, and I might safely have travelled on it all the time. Not a single change have I yet discovered in the new one—not even in the advertisements.

One of the last discoveries we make in the front office of the *Fonda del Norte* is a stair leading out of a corner into the upper regions. We follow it exploringly, and have just groped our way to the first landing when a door opens, and a smart-looking young woman, with a great show of white linen on her breast, comes out of a room. At the mention of eating she grasps the situation at once, and re-opening the door she came out of, she ushers us into a *salle-à-manger*, with the comforting assurance that dinner will be ready in *cinco minute*. Textually *cinco minute* means five minutes, but practically it signifies anything from a week to a century. It is first cousin to that other celebrated deceiver, the Highlandman's " bittock." That *salle-à-manger* admitted by its own clock in the corner of the room that I entered it exactly at half-past six. A long table reaching from the door to the fireplace at the upper end was already laid, and the smart young woman was giving it its finishing touches. But the finishing it needed! Irish estimates on a sultry night, and with Tim Healy in his war-paint, were a flash of lightning compared with it. The señorita had arranged to her satisfaction the glass, the napkins, and the knives and forks. She had artistically grouped all down the centre of the table wine-bottles in threes and fours—here champagne, here Burgundy, and farther on Valdepena. Beside every group she had put a wine-list, and in the centre there was a revolving pyramid, a perfect wine trophy, on which she concentrated her most famous *crus*.

When done, this *tour de force* of decoration evidently gave her no small satisfaction. She looked at it up the table, then down the table, and across the table from each corner. Feeling sure that it would stand criticism, she went out and brought in the cook in his white jacket and cap. He admired it enthusiastically, and then the two of them went out on a balcony to look up and down the street. Nobody happened to be in the street except a donkey carrying two bags of charcoal in panniers, but the prospect was exciting enough to detain the señorita and the cook for a good five minutes. He returned to his kitchen, and she leaned her arms on the back of a chair in order to think out the next move in the campaign. Evidently she hesitated between bringing in the bread or the water carafes. After three minutes' reflection by the clock she decided on doing the water first. A dozen half-empty carafes left over from breakfast still stood on the table. She brought in a huge pitcher and filled them up where they stood without any cleaning or rearranging. This entitled her to another two minutes on the balcony, where the donkey and the bags of charcoal still formed the entire view. On her next visit to the back regions she returned with a basket full of rolls and chunks of bread. Making another round of the table, she dropped one into each napkin and took a fresh survey of her handiwork.

By this time her *cinco-minute* had stretched out to half an hour, and the short hand of the clock in the corner pointed to seven. Here the cook sauntered in again, but not on business. He, too, had become interested in the donkey and the charcoal, and going to another balcony—there were three in the room—his eyes lingered fondly on them for several minutes. Meanwhile the señorita was calmly collecting her wine carafes—the wine of the country, which is never charged for in Spain, because, we presume, it carries its own punishment with it. She carried out an armful of empty ones, and in due time brought them back full.

When they were dumped on the table it might have been thought that the preliminaries of the *table d'hôte* were concluded—but not by a long way. Not a bell had rung yet, and it needs a great deal of bell-ringing to start anything in Spain, whether it be Mass, or dinner, or a railway train. At half-past seven a bell broke loose somewhere below, and for three minutes made an awful clatter. It ought to have brought in a rush of hungry diners, but its only immediate result was a lady of uncertain age, but very definite temper, who came in looking hungry, though by no means hopeful. She dropped languidly into a chair, and seizing the official railway time-table, became engrossed in its enthralling contents. In her wake came a *caballero*, a very stout man, with a florid face, half covered with a moustache, which seemed to be the delight of his life. He was an old hand, and merely took a provisional survey, the results of which not being altogether satisfactory, he dodged out again.

Another wearisome interval of ten, or it might have been twelve minutes, was passed by the señorita in struggling with three gasaliers, which she ultimately got lighted. This was the signal for a second fit of bell-ringing, violent enough for an alarm of fire. But the only person it alarmed was a sallow-faced youth, in Dundreary whiskers as black as sloes. He came in mincing and smiling, with a special squint in the corner of his eye for the señorita, who responded disdainfully—Romeo's account for last week being still to settle perchance. We were grateful to the sallow-faced youth, however, for sitting down at table, and giving us an excuse for doing the same. A third bell rang, and it meant business, for the soup soon followed it. The señorita's five minutes, which had begun at half-past six, lasted till exactly a quarter to eight. Everything comes to him who waits—even in Burgos.

SALAMANCA.

ONE cannot say he has been in Spain until he has seen Salamanca. He may miss Santander, and it might not fatally injure his reputation as a traveller were he to see Burgos only from the railway train. At the same time, I can assure him that, apart from the cathedral and its Murillos, Burgos is well worth stopping at. But there is no option left him as to doing Salamanca. That is where old Spain survives in its purest form, and where the essential picturesqueness of Spanish life can be best appreciated. What need also to recall to any Englishman the glorious traditions of Salamanca in the Peninsular War? In the triumphal march of Wellington from the west to the Pyrenees, Salamanca is one of the brightest milestones. For itself alone it would be worth travelling all the distance to see. As a short offshoot of fifty or sixty miles from the main line to Madrid, it is a light day's work. The junction station is Medina, about 200 kilomètres (120 miles) north of Madrid. From it three or four cross lines radiate, marking it out for an important centre in the system. Besides the Salamanca line, which has now become part of a through route into Portugal, there is one to Zamora and another to Avila.

The express train starting from Paris at eight o'clock in the evening reaches Medina about midnight next day. You can then either sleep at Medina, and go on by an early train in the morning, or you can take the connecting night train, which reaches Salamanca at four o'clock in the morning. Four o'clock is not a very comfortable hour in most countries, but it never comes amiss to a Spaniard. He regards it as a most respectable hour for going to bed. Do not be surprised, therefore, if all the hotel omnibuses in Salamanca are waiting for you at the station. They will be drawn up in a line just outside — half-a-dozen of them, great hulking vehicles, each one fit to hold all the Salamanca passengers in the train. Four of the half-dozen will probably go back empty, but they will be quite as cheerful as if they were full, and they will all come back again to the next train smiling. It was evidently to oblige them that the railway company dropped the station down on a ridge about a mile and a half from the town. It might have been as easily placed quite close to the town, for the line afterwards passes within a stone's-throw of the two cathedrals.

Another characteristic example of Spanish conservatism. Even the *ferro carril* could not be per-

mitted to kill off ancient institutions. Work had
to be found for the mules and the diligences that
were frozen off the road. The diligences were accordingly cut down into 'buses, and the mules had
still the pleasure of bumping them about on the
cobbles as in the brave days of old. But you will
be richly repaid for your bumping if you chance,
as I have done, on a genuine old-fashioned Spanish
fonda — hotels they are beginning to call them
now—but your modern hotel could be cut out of
them in slices, and never be missed. The mon-
astic masons who built the cathedrals, and put
sometimes twenty feet of solid stonework into their
walls, seem to have condescended now and then
to fill up their spare time with a *fonda*. They
planned them in cathedral style, and were liberal
in space as well as in solidity. The trifles which
architects waste their thoughts on nowadays—how
to get the greatest number of rooms out of their
cubic area, and to make the rooms fit together
neatly—were beneath their notice. If they had an
odd corner they could not turn to account they
simply left it alone, and often a very good use was
found for it afterwards. If when their outer rooms
had been planned they found a few dark bits in
the centre which they could not light—why, there
was always timber enough to fill them. Moreover, they gave a soothing dimness to the interior,
and made shadows which were very welcome when
the sun was indulging in a noontide blaze.

Six weeks of Salamanca heat would burn

through the walls of our Hotels Metropoles and
Victorias.   It would be almost impossible to sleep
or eat in them.   But however scorching a day it
may be outside, there ·is always coolness and re-
pose in a *fonda.*   The walls are stone built, and
window-sills four feet deep show that there must
be some substance to them.   Attached to every
window is a thick wooden shutter, which opens
and closes along with it.   In the mornings and
evenings the whole barricade is thrown wide open,
and during the day it is closed.   The temperature
is thus always kept much lower than that of the
outer air.   That is the secret of comfortable living
in a hot climate, and the old *fonda* builders knew
it.   With their massive walls and darkened interiors
they could defy the sun.   From the wide stone-
paved porch to the farthest corridor on the top
floor they studied coolness first and appearance
afterwards.   In this way appearance is not sacri-
ficed, for there may be a truer beauty in plainness
which perfectly serves its purpose than in florid
ornament which has no serviceable purpose at all.

A person of healthy taste cannot be half an hour
in one of these grim old *fondas* without beginning
to like them.   Enclosed and shut in by them,
there is a kind of life peculiar to themselves and
of a piece all through.   You would be surprised to
see anybody hurrying about in them as having
anything to do which might not be equally well
done to-morrow or next week.   You would be
shocked to meet a man on the old stone stairs

rushing up three or four steps at a time. You might be there for months without hearing any one ask to be called in the morning. If you were to live half a century on the premises you could not find out what are supposed to be the meal hours. In the eating-room there is always a fully laid table, with napkins, glasses, carafes of wine, and other seductive decorations in full trim. It looks as if something were to be on at once, and you may hang about in the hope of hearing a bell ring, but you will wait in vain. Spanish meals never come when they are expected. They invest themselves in the supplementary pleasure of a continual surprise. Only one thing about them you may be quite sure of, that when you are most impatient they are least disposed to be hurried.

By degrees it dawned upon me as an exquisite joke that the venerable *fonda* should ever have come into contact with railways at all. It is putting new wine into old bottles with a vengeance. The *fonda*, however, troubles itself just as little as possible about its new partner. It keeps no time-table, does not know when trains arrive or start, but has an impression that they make their time to suit the *fonda* omnibuses. That may easily be, for the Salamanca railway administration is very obliging for Spain. It does not expect you to travel in the heat of the day, all its trains being in the morning or the evening. When one does start, it gives the whole population along the road a fair chance to get some fun out of it. If he cannot travel himself, he may come to the station and get all the news of the day from those who do. It is a British delusion that railways are not popular in Spain. Figaro is no longer a barber; he has taken to engine-driving or conducting, and his opportunities of disseminating news have multiplied a hundred-fold. The Spaniards are really fond of railways, so far as they can be fitted into Spanish tastes and habits.

IN A SPANISH PLAY-BOOTH.

THE average Spaniard is passionately fond of the play, at least as passionately as he can be of anything outside of his own fantasy. Perhaps it is because it feeds and influences his fantasy that he is so fervid a playgoer. While the Portuguese have a weakness for newspapers—there are sixty daily papers of one kind or another published in Lisbon — the Spaniard cannot have theatres enough. In Madrid their name is legion ; and in the large provincial cities they are increasing fast with the prosperity of the people. Even in the south, in sunny Andalusia, where the bull-ring is the ruling recreation, the theatres begin to make some headway against it. If ever the horrible bull-ring is killed at all, it will be by the stage rather than by either the Church or the Press.

As yet Spanish theatres are more remarkable for quantity than for quality. There are many grades of them, from the *Teatro Real*, which is the Lyceum of its district, down to the strolling booth,

C

which combine all the piquancies of a music-hall and a variety-show. In Spain there seem to be no difficulties about full licence and half licence, such as vex the managerial soul in London. I am not sure that a theatre here needs any licence at all, but, judging from their programmes, they can do almost anything they choose to. The travelling companies, of which there are many, and some of them noted all through the Peninsula, practise quite a unique kind of art. They keep up the good old native drama as it has been played from the days of Cervantes downward, but in deference to modern taste they tack on at the end a vaudeville more or less spicy. While in Zaffra, my overwhelmingly kind entertainer asked in joke if I would like to see a native play of the country. I told him that, next to the first sight of a new Rio Tinto, nothing would please me better. So after dinner—which is an eight o'clock function in Spain—we started off. It was a little past nine, the regular hour for the play to begin here, but there seemed to be little fear of our being late.

Our local guide led us through one narrow street after another, pointing out here a convent and there a *casino*, all shrouded in darkness, broken only by an oil lamp or two twinkling through the open door. After five minutes of this he brought us out on the *plaza*, a fine broad square, arcaded round with heavy massive pillars. But the theatre was not in this fashionable quarter

We had to plunge again into the winding lanes, keeping close to the sides of the houses, where there was generally a little strip of smooth pavement. Suddenly we stepped out of the deepening shadows into a great glow of moonlight. We were in the *Campo de Seville*, the Champ de Mars of Zaffra. Right in the centre of it was a large booth—the unmistakable object of our quest. Of its kind it was a very fair "fit up," the walls being of wood, and evidently well put together. In shape it was not the usual circus or horse-shoe, but a plain rectangle, the auditorium being much longer than its breadth. It might have been as much as 200 feet from the door to the proscenium, and wooden benches filled the whole area. They were the select part of the house, for which the fee was one *peseta*, or franc. The cheap parts were in the galleries running down either side, where, for about threepence, a three hours' entertainment could be enjoyed. The one entrance for the whole house was at the end of the booth, and the stage was hermetically shut off at the other. All communications between the front and behind had to be carried on by stage-whispers at the side of the curtain.

In accordance with the enlightened and liberal ideas which now prevail in fashionable theatres, programmes were distributed free. At least you think so when you get one handed to you with a bow which would do credit to an ambassador. When you look at it, however, .you find that it

is for *to-morrow night.* To-night's programmes
were given out yesterday, and are now, of course,
at a premium. There is a wrinkle for some of the
sixpenny programme houses in the neighbourhood
of Charing Cross! By special favour we got a
bill for the evening—a long strip of paper rather
nicely printed, and well set off with catch headings.
Don Quixote might have written the grandiose
opening, which, literally done into English, was
thus :—

THEATRE OF VARIETIES,

SITUATED IN THE CAMPO DE SEVILLE.

By the Comic Lyric Company, under the direction of the
leading Actor,

DON RICHARD MELA.

Grand and Varied Function for Saturday, the 6th July 1889.

The Popular Drama of Andalusian Customs,
in Four Acts, entitled

DIEGO CORRIENTES;

OR, THE MAGNANIMOUS BANDIT.

At the eleventh hour, however, the stage manager seemed to have changed his mind about "The
Magnanimous Bandit." He may have thought it
too good to throw away on a half-empty house—
the benches were indeed but sparsely occupied—
and something else had been substituted, evidently
a domestic drama of love and passion, the same
all the world over. The leading lady, a somewhat
buxom beauty, with raven black hair and a killing
eye, has reached a crisis in her life. She has

hooked a marquis or a duke, who, in the evening-dress of a waiter, goes prancing in and out, every time in a greater hurry, to get her to go to the altar. But she has a good deal of preliminary discussion to go through with a melancholy old woman, no doubt her duenna, and a billiard-marker-looking youth who knows more than is convenient of her antecedents. Whether by accident or secret design of the billiard-marker, her exit for the purpose of visiting the church and making the impatient duke a happy man is interrupted by two new arrivals—an old man, who claims her as his long-lost daughter, and a pert girl in search of a mother. She disowns the humble but virtuous peasant in the red sash and brilliantly checked trousers, whereupon he lets loose on her a storm of paternal entreaties and reproaches.

At the height of the row there is a fierce ring at the bell, and the waiter-like duke bounces in for the third and last time to ask if his Dulcinea is coming to church or not. In the excitement of the moment she appeals to the old man as *padre* to have mercy on her and help her out of the mess. The dear old name *padre*, though it slipped out unawares, brings down the relentless parent, who vamps up a transparent yarn to deceive the duke. But let us jump to the finale, lest the description become as wearisome as the play itself. In the last act Dulcinea learns that the pert girl, who has been saying nasty things to her

all the time, is her long-lost daughter. Where the
long-lost father may be is of no consequence.
Father, daughter, and grandchild having in this
miraculous way found each other again, all hug
each other on the stage, and resolve to return to
their humble home, and leave the now furious
duke to prance about in his marble halls without
his napkin under his arm.

If the play itself was dull, the by-play was
amusing enough. The prompter was an entertainment in himself. He did not wait, as he has to
do in other countries, till a necessity arose for his
services, but he took for granted that nobody knew
a word of his part, and gabbled every line straight
on, keeping a sentence or two ahead of the actor.
He spoke in a sing-song stage-whisper, perfectly
audible, I should think, even at the back of the
house. I had the misfortune to be well forward,
and got a great deal more of the prompter than of
anybody else. What was maddening at first became a novel amusement when taken philosophically. I soon found myself comparing the prompter's sonorous prelude with the confused echoes
which followed on the stage. Many of the effects
were very comical. The leading lady took it most
coolly, repeating every phrase exactly as it came
from the wings. The old father was less phleg-
matic, and made an occasional attempt to get
ahead on his own account. But in doing so he
only excited the prompter to a more vigorous and
more audible initiation. He was not to be shaken

off anyhow. In the heat of the contest the actor and he would gabble together for a minute or two, but the prompter was longer winded, and had the advantage of being able to go straight ahead. He always came out a winner, and recovered his normal lead of a sentence or a sentence and a half.

In the refreshment department there was also some good fun—for the spectator, I mean, not for the caterer. The bar was a little counter set up in a corner on one side of the proscenium. It was presided over by one Hebe, with two boys to do the running. Either her selection of drinks was imperfect, or the play was too emotional, for the thirst of the audience was almost *nil*. More business was done with the back of the stage than the front. Soon after the curtain dropped at the end of an act, a hand would be thrust through the side of it. Hebe would give a tumbler to one of the boys to put into the hand, on which it would be gently drawn in again. Dulcinea may have sent round for a lemonade to cool her, or the *padre* may have needed a gin-sling to brace him up after his tempest of paternal agony. Anyhow, the players were the best customers of the bar. Poor players! Let us hope that before the tour ends *pesetas* may be more plentiful, and tears less difficult to draw, than Dulcinea and her old father found them to be.

MADRID.

THE Spaniards are not proud of their capital as Englishmen are of London, or Frenchmen of Paris. They admit that it has few natural beauties or advantages, and that the attractions, such as they are, have had for the most part to be created for it. Like a plain woman, it requires a deal of dressing up, and has to put on forced airs of gaiety. Force of practice is, however, becoming a second nature with it. Madrid is gradually asserting itself as one of the gay capitals of Europe. What with rebuilding, landscape-gardening, and *al fresco* entertainments peculiar to the country, it is fast outgrowing its original sombreness. The Madrid season, which opens with the first frosts of October, and winds up gloriously with the Carnival, begins to attract visitors from across the Pyrenees. To pleasure-seekers it is an interesting variation on Paris or Monte Carlo. They can have in it all these fashionable frivolities served up with a new and more piquant flavour. The Madrileno is a

more interesting entertainer than the prover-
bially polite Frenchman. His grave courtesy is
not so wearisome as the eternal bowing and grim-
acing of his northern neighbours. At heart he is
quite as gay a dog, but in his fastest moments he
never forgets his native dignity.

The Madrilenos are children of the sun, and
without the *Puerto del Sol* there could be no
Madrid ; but they equally enjoy the soothing
shadows of night. An ideal life means to them
breakfast about mid-day, lounging or driving all
afternoon in the Prado, dinner at eight or nine
o'clock, theatre from ten till past midnight, and
political discussion in a *café* till nearly sunrise.
Odd that of all the capitals the one which has least
serious work to do should spend the longest time
over it. But Madrid has made fashions and
customs to suit itself. Like an experienced co-
quette, it knows exactly the light and the colour
which set it off best. Under a blaze of gas, or a
galaxy of electric lamps, its long bare streets become picturesque. Even dead walls may be made
beautiful by a judicious arrangement of shadows.
The Madrileno's love of display has much to do
with his social habits, but the sanitary conditions
of the town also necessitate the largest possible
amount of open - air life. If the four hundred
thousand people in Madrid were shut up in their
own houses as Londoners are for more than half
of their existence, death would soon be welcomed
as an agreeable change. The mortality is bad

enough as it is—about forty-five per thousand it is said, which is fully double the London rate—but then it would be worse than New Orleans or Vera Cruz. It is the amount of time which can be spent in the open air that makes life possible at all.

Opinions may differ as to whether this be a misfortune or otherwise. The Madrileno himself evidently thinks it is otherwise. He has cheerfully shaped and moulded his existence to suit the circumstances. They enable him to reduce his domestic expenditure to a minimum. Even in good society he may get on with a very modest domestic establishment. Furniture of the plainest and scantiest will serve his turn ; but if he is to cut a figure on the Prado, he must have a smart equipage; his horses must be of the best Andalusian blood ; his coachman must look as if he were fresh from Rotten Row or the Bois de Boulogne ; and his own tailoring must be well up to date. More than half the income of fashionable Madrid is spent at the theatre, the bull-ring, and the Prado. These are the three local luxuries which swallow up all else. In order to atone for them, the severest economy is practised in every other department. When a young couple are planning matrimony in Madrid, the anxious question with them is not what it will cost to keep house, but how a brougham and a fur-tippeted coachman are to be financed out of three thousand *pesetas*, or a hundred and fifty pounds a-year.

Foreign visitors can afford to judge charitably
this love of display, which seems to be inborn in
the Madrileno. It is certainly not an unamiable
quality, however indiscreet and improvident it may
be. Showy people are invariably hospitable, and
the hospitality of Madrid has passed into a proverb.
It must have a deeper root than vanity, though
vanity, doubtless, gives a sharper zest to it. From
a public point of view it may be good tactics.
Madrid having few charms of its own to attract
foreigners, must have them provided artificially.
Its only natural charm is its climate, and even that
is subject to such trifling drawbacks as biting east
winds and sharp frosts. But for them life in Madrid
would be always endurable, and often delicious.
It has the valuable secret of being distinctive.
There is a great deal in it not to be found in Paris,
or even Vienna. Modelled though it be on the
conventional continental capital, it has preserved
much national spirit and originality. French
modes can never efface the true Spaniard. Beneath
them all he retains a dignity and a chivalrous
grace all his own.

Many writers, including the author of 'Murray's
Handbook of Spain,' have reckoned it among
Spain's misfortunes that Madrid should have been
selected for the capital. They say truly that it
had little claim to such distinction, and few
qualifications for it. The real origin of its choice
was a gouty whim of Charles the Fifth, who fancied
that its bracing air suited him better than the other

headquarters of his Court at Valladolid, Granada, Seville, or Toledo. Compared with these it had neither historical interest nor physical attraction. The only public argument for it was its being supposed to be the geographical centre of the Peninsula. Captious critics have questioned even that, but tradition concedes it, and the point is hardly worth contesting minutely. Madrid may plead with greater effect that if it was a bad choice, other capitals have been equally ill chosen, and yet have served their purpose fairly well. · In Europe at least, it has not been the rule, but the exception, for a capital to be well located. Berlin, which has the highest destiny of them all, owes less to nature than Madrid itself; and St Petersburg differs from Madrid only in having been built on a swamp instead of on a wind-swept plateau. The founders of Washington have been the butt of endless satire about streets losing themselves in bogs, or being laid out so as to best catch the full force of blizzards ; in spite of which Washington flourishes, and will soon be the social as well as the political centre of the States.

There are precedents, and important ones, for hoping that Madrid will outlive its drawbacks and become a capital worthy of Spain. So far it has been no drag on the national development, but in certain events it may have been a safeguard. If Charles the Fifth, or one of his immediate successors, had raised Toledo, Valladolid, Seville, or any of the old historical cities to metropolitan rank, there would have been unquenchable jealousy and heartburning among all the others. If in the many civil wars which Spain has gone through, faction had been intensified by local rivalry, the struggle for life would have been tenfold more severe. The comparative neutrality of the seat of Government, combined with its central position, has undoubtedly been of strategic value. A more picturesque capital Spain might easily have had, and one in stronger historical sympathy with the nation ; but these advantages could have been got only at a high price, and Charles the Fifth's prosaic choice was, taken all round, probably the best that could have been made.

CORTES AND ITS LEADERS.

FOR several months to come Spain and Spanish finance will have to be considerably in evidence. The storm which has been long gathering over the heads of the present Liberal Ministry broke in the Cortes last session, and is raging still. The Conservatives found their opportunity to attack, and did it with such unexpected vigour, that at one moment their success seemed possible. Señor Sagasta has, however, defended himself no less vigorously, and the issue still hangs in the balance. But that is for the moment only. Even if Ministers should pull through the present crisis and get the Cortes adjourned, their fate will be only postponed. It is merely a question whether they go out now or hang on for another five or six months. The chances are, perhaps, rather in favour of their being able to hang on, as Señor Canovas is shrewd enough not to grasp at power until he sees a good chance of being able to hold it. He has the rare virtue among Spanish politicians of patience, and will not spoil his game by forcing it prematurely.

But there are deeper questions in agitation than a change of Ministry : it is felt by intelligent Spaniards that a change of system is also wanted. The country has had politics enough of the party-fighting and office-hunting kind. It has got as much political freedom and privilege as any community need wish for. Señor Castelar himself could not give it an additional right, but would be more likely to chafe under the exercise of those it already enjoys. As between moderate Conservative and moderate Republican, it is only tweedledum and tweedledee. Thanks to the self-devotion and the sagacity of the Queen on the one hand, and to the chivalry of the nation on the other, the dynasty is more secure to-day than it has been at any other time in the present century. In creating this situation the Queen has rendered a historical service to Europe as well as to Spain. A distracted and divided Spain would have been a European evil, while a united and contented Spain is one more safeguard of peace. For the first time in this generation Spaniards can now proceed to the long-delayed development of the country. They have had enough of constitution-mongering, and now they want administration.

But where are the administrators? There are many able men in the Cortes—brilliant speakers, skilful tacticians, and no doubt zealous patriots ;

but of statesmen who can administer with a will of
their own very few have yet come to the front.
Many have tried their hands at finance without
proving Goschens, or even fair press copies of
Mr Childers ; and we could not have anything
much fainter than that to be readable at all.   In
the long array of Presidents of the Council, only
Sagasta in the one camp and Canovas in the other
have exhibited the moral ascendancy which gives
real control over the governing machine.   They
alone have dominated their ministerial colleagues
and their party.   But much more of the same kind
of domination will be needed in order to give
Spain what she most sorely needs — a capable
administrative authority at the head of affairs—
one which will transact business in a business-like
way, and will see that all its subordinates do the
same.

In her government, as well as in her railway
administration, the crying want of Spain is expedition.   Years are spent over affairs which ought to
be put through in as many weeks, and twenty officials are half-paid for doing badly work that one
well-paid competent man would do much better
and quicker.   This is especially true of business
affecting foreigners.   I could give many curious
illustrations of it, but they may come in better
later on.   They need only be referred to now as
bearing on the feebleness of the administrative
instinct in the Spanish public service.   What
would not a man like President Diaz, of Mexico,

be worth to Spain, with his faculty of discussing important transactions face to face with either native or foreigner, and, after ten minutes' conversation, giving a decision which will be carried out to the letter! When President Diaz came into power he was resolved in his own mind that Mexico should be opened up, and that his life-work would be to do it. He has done it, and, thanks not only to his patriotic courage, but to his rare business faculty, Mexico has made greater progress in the past three or four years than Spain has done in thirty.

Had the late King Alfonso been spared, he might have become another such ruler as President Diaz. He had a passion for all practical subjects of administration, and had also the courage of his opinions. He was free, too, from the dread of responsibility, which makes Spanish Ministers and officials fear to put their signatures to anything if they can avoid it. The Queen may, and does, observe admirably all constitutional forms; but she cannot be expected to go into departmental details, and take a personal initiative in matters of concession or contract. With a Prime Minister who could do that for her, and who could cut away at a stroke several miles of the red tape which strangles every public department, she would be a perfect ruler. The hour has come for such a man, and, whoever he may be, he will find a great occasion waiting for him. The fortune of Spain depends just now on his speedy appearance,

D

and no doubt he will show up one of these days.
The Conservatives are confident that they already
possess him in their leader, Canovas, and certainly
the business men of Madrid all speak highly of
him.

Canovas, or some other man of strong backbone
and limited jaw, at the head of a like-minded
Cabinet, might do wonders here in a short time.
He might even achieve the hitherto hopeless feat
of balancing the Budget, and that would put
another complexion on Spanish credit. The present is really a Budget crisis, though that phase of
the difficulty is kept discreetly in the background.
It is the skeleton which both sides tacitly agree to
leave alone in the cupboard as much as possible.
The present Finance Minister has virtually lost his
chance of dealing effectively with it. His Budget
not having been voted within the statutory period
—by June 30—that of the last financial year continues in force. Root-and-branch measures are
not in his line, and were not expected from him.
He owes his position really to the *haute finance,*
who have the heavy end of the floating debt to
carry. While it suits them to make things endurable for him — and they do it by lending him
money at 3 or 4 per cent—the financial crisis will
not become acute. Gratitude has, of course, to be
shown in other ways, and as everything turns on
finance, the high financiers are *de facto* governing
Spain. They may not be getting all they would
like, but they have the best of what is going.

In the event of a change of Government, finance would still be the crucial problem. The Conservatives have yet to find two primary requisites of office—a majority in the Cortes, and a good understanding with the bankers who control the floating debt. The breaking up of the Liberal majority into factions gives them a chance of securing the first, and the second would naturally follow, for bankers like to be on the side of the big battalions. Even the Liberals are inclined to admit that the other side should now have an innings; and a Conservative Cabinet is one of the possibilities of the next few months.

IN THE SIERRA MORENA.

THE Monasteria de los Angelos is one of the holy places of Catholic Spain. The monks who inhabited it gave the olive-clad hill on which it stands the attractive name of the Hill of the Angels, and it is worthy of the title. Now that the monks themselves have disappeared, the angels remain, for a lovelier spot is not to be seen in Southern Spain, or one more characteristic of the country. The monastery buildings are perched on a grassy platform which commands miles and miles of a view over a sea of mountains. In every direction hill and valley succeed each other as far as the eye can reach. Some of the hills are dark and frowning, ribbed with granite to their tops ; others reflect the glowing greens of chestnut woods and the dark purple of olive groves. In the hollows below nestle villages, on whose red-tiled roofs and whitewashed walls the sun seems to beat in vain : however hot its glare, they always look cool and pleasant.

At first glance these hills might be mistaken

for wild, uncultivated country ; but they are one of the richest and most productive parts of Spain. The simple, hard-working peasants who occupy it maintain the arts of cultivation which were bequeathed to them by the Moors. They are substantially the same as when the Moors left them— industrious in their way, poetic, dreamy, and shut up in a little world of their own. But there is a good deal more in them than they have got credit for : like their country, they have been undervalued. Since better opportunities were offered them they have wakened up, and with very little training they have become intelligent, reliable workmen. In the past two or three years the Sierra Morena, from being the most backward and least-known part of Spain, has changed to the most progressive. Its transformation began with the opening of the Zafra-Huelva Railway, which crosses the range from north to south, giving its hitherto sealed-up valleys an outlet to the coast at Huelva, the great copper port of the Peninsula. It also places them in direct connection with the vast wheat plains of Estramadura, which stretch from the north side of the Sierra Morena away to the Portuguese frontier. What has been known from the days of the Romans as the granary of Spain, can now freely exchange its cereals for the fruit grown in the boundless orchards and gardens of the Sierra.

From time immemorial the peasants of the Sierra Morena have been distinguished fruit-

growers. They have strawberries very nearly all
the year round. Their cherries are the sweetest
and most prolific in Spain. Their chestnut-trees,
though hundreds of years old, yield as abundantly
as ever. Their cork-trees are also veterans, and
every time they are stripped the thicker is the
skin taken off them. Cork-making is one of the
ancient industries of the Sierra, and the railway
has given it a fresh impetus. Cheaper transport
will enable it to compete more successfully with
the cork-forests of Morocco, the production of
which is unlimited. At one of the stations on the
Zafra-Huelva line a cork-cutting factory is now
being erected, which will bring improved methods
to bear on the industry. Hitherto it has been
conducted in a hand-to-mouth fashion. The
owners of the cork-trees lease them at so much a
year to the merchants, who keep men continually
employed watching and stripping them. It takes
seven years to renew the skin, and the older the
tree the thicker the cork. The largest forests lie
toward the Portuguese side of the Sierra. On the
Seville side the cork-trees grow indiscriminately
with chestnuts and olives.

The enchanting scenery and the fruitful gardens
of the Sierra Morena are the smallest of its dis-
tinctions. It is also the centre of Spain's mineral
wealth. From the platform of this Monasteria de
los Angelos, looking southward, may be seen the
smoke of the Rio Tinto, the Tharsis, and half-a-
dozen other historical mines. In a clear day the

mines themselves may be faintly distinguished, though, as the crow flies, the Rio Tinto is nearly twenty miles distant, and the Tharsis still further. Away to the right are several French mines, also rising into importance ; and in every valley there is the possibility of new discoveries, which may eclipse even the Tinto itself. In the immediate neighbourhood of the Tinto the chances are now small, for that area has been thoroughly prospected ; but north of it there are miles of virgin country, the secrets of which have yet to be unlocked. They need not be confined to copper, for that is only one of many mineral treasures which abound in the Sierra. On the hills round about Huelva there are scores of manganese mines, which have been worked for years in a small way. Their combined output makes a very considerable export from Huelva.

North of the manganese deposits come the copper, and beyond these again are silver mines. Only a few are being worked as yet, though it is in silver that the next great development of the Sierra is likely to be made. There are records of silver mines having been worked here before the opening up of Mexico. Philip II. ordered some of them to be closed, in order to force the miners to go to Mexico. Local tradition has preserved their memory, and measures are already in progress for restarting some of them. Doubtless they have also furnished a clue to many new finds which are being carefully nursed until the proper time

arrives for their development. One prospecting
syndicate has been particularly active, its operations extending all over the Sierra, even further
north than Zafra. It is directed by Messrs Sundheim and Doetsch, the founders of the Rio Tinto
Company, and the original purchasers of the
property from the Spanish Government. Both
of them German settlers in Spain, they have done
more for the growth of the country than any living
native, be he politician, miner, or merchant. How
they secured the Rio Tinto and put it in the way
of becoming the greatest mine in the world, will be
told further on. That brilliant *coup* was but the
beginning of a series of splendid enterprises which
are still in full swing.

They designed and built the two principal railways in the province—the first from Huelva to
Seville, which now forms part of the Rothschild
system, and the second from Huelva across the
Sierra to Estramadura. Their special work at
present is creating traffic for the new line. They
are opening up marble quarries on the mountains
which will supply the finest building and decor-
ative stone within reach of either London, Paris, or
Madrid. Many thousand tons of white marble
are now lying in blocks ready to be brought down
to Huelva as soon as the sawing and polishing
works are in operation. The coloured marble,
which was largely used on the railway for bridge-
work and facing tunnels, is in a less forward state ;
but it too will be in the market in a few months.

Simultaneously their prospecting syndicate has been on the look-out all over the Sierra for new mines. Its superintending engineer, Herr Blum, was the first mining-engineer of the Rio Tinto, and started it on its marvellous career of prosperity. He has his headquarters at the marble quarries at Fuenteheridos, where he lives the life of a stoical philosopher, enthroned among mining schemes and specimens of all sorts of minerals, from gold to iron. The only mineral he has not yet struck in the Sierra is the one he would best like to see—coal; but he does not despair of finding it still. It would make the fortune of Spain, and raise it from the poorest to one of the richest countries in Europe.

HUELVA.

Spain is less patronised by tourists than any other country in Europe. That may not be wholly a disadvantage for Spain, as some tourists can make themselves anything but good company; but it is a paradox which deserves the attention of Mr Cook and other professors of the art of personally-conducted travelling. Why should Spain, of all countries, be avoided even by the most persevering of globe-trotters? No one will say that it is commonplace and not worth visiting. The scenery cannot be objected to, for the beauties of the Pyrenees only dawn fully on you when you cross the Spanish frontier, and the orange-groves of Andalusia are as sweet to the eye as those of Sorrento. It cannot be reproached with lack of historical interest, for every step you take should thrill you with the memories and traditions of centuries. Vitoria, Torres Vedras, and Badajoz will never again be to Englishmen the sleepy old towns they are in reality. The gloomy grandeur of the Escurial blends itself in imagination with the crisis of the Spanish Armada.

And when you get to the south a whole heroic age can be conjured up. The bull-fights of Seville are a direct survival of the Roman games. The cathedral of Cordova is the greatest of Moorish mosques, remaining still in many parts exactly as the Moors left it. Less known, but more memorable than all else together, is the little monastery at the Rabida in Huelva Bay, from which Columbus sailed, with three small vessels, to discover the New World. This, one would expect to find the most venerated and frequented shrine of the sightseer. Every American, from Hudson's Bay to Cape Horn, should have his eyes turned towards it as a place of pilgrimage, and even for *blasé* Europeans it should have at least as much interest as Geneva or the Castle of Chillon. The Rabida, however, is no show-place, and the old monastery on the hill which changed the destiny of the world is strangely neglected, both by poet, painter, and traveller. Its principal visitors are a few peasants now and then from the vicinity, and a peasant like themselves shows them through it. He leads them from corridor to corridor, pointing out the cell in which the great navigator lived while he was the guest of his friends the monks, the room in which his plans of the voyage were discussed with chart and compass on the table, and the chapel where a farewell Mass was said for him and his brave comrades.

Having gazed reverently on it all, the sunburnt peasants return home proud of the man who conferred such glory on their country, and especially on their dear province of Huelva. It matters little to them that few foreigners should seek to share their worship of Christopher Columbus and the old monastery of the Rabida ; but still, in an age when people will run so far for a new sensation, it is puzzling. If it could be said in excuse that Huelva was an out-of-the-way place, difficult to reach, and harder still to live in when one got there, that would be a sort of reason, or at least excuse. But nothing could be further from the mark than both assumptions. Huelva by railway is not farther from London than Pesth, and it has a great advantage over Pesth in possessing two alternative routes by sea. The voyage can be made direct in a Rio Tinto steamer in five days and a half, or by mail - steamer to Lisbon, and thence by coaster or by rail overland.

For a show-place Huelva is exceptionally easy of access. But what about the living ? will be the next inquiry of the personally-conducted who hesitates to leave the beaten track. He is particularly sceptical about Spain, for there is a popular legend —how it arose heaven knows—that Spanish hotels are like most other Spanish institutions—greatly behind the age. Their cooking is supposed to maintain the partiality of Sancho Panza for oil and garlic ; their beds are alleged to be very much over-populated ; and their bedroom furniture to be of Moorish severity and scantiness. It is wonderful how long-lived travellers' tales can be. Nothing is harder to kill, unless it be the reputation of a good man who does not deserve it. Doubtless many Spanish hotels of the old type still exist, and their customers very probably continue to be well satisfied with them. The fastidious traveller seldom need risk his precious person in them, however. Even in second or third rate towns in the Peninsula the fashionable hotel mania has made rapid progress. Madrid has a few hostelries of the new style, which can put up from a hundred to a hundred and thirty guests, with all the comfort and even luxury of London or Paris. But there is still room in Madrid for a really first-class establishment like the Metropole or the Paris Continental. The best of the existing houses are only good, and they are very dear in proportion to what they give for the money. In the provinces there are houses much more reasonable in their charges.

The best hotel in the Peninsula I found in a very unexpected spot, and I have hardly yet got over my surprise that such a palatial establishment should be so little known. The Colon or Colombus Hotel is one of the sights, as well as one of the institutions, of Huelva. In size, in arrangement, in furniture, and above all in *cuisine*, it is the best I have met with in Spain, or in fact south of Paris. The Rothschilds, the Rio Tinto Company, the two local railways—Seville-Huelva, and Zafra-Huelva—were all at the founding of it; so if they

could not produce a model hotel, from whom is one
to be expected?   It is situated in the outskirts of
the town, well up the bay, and near what will ultimately be the principal water front.   There are
four distinct blocks enclosing a quadrangle of an
acre or two in extent.   The front block is divided
into suites of apartments, of which there are fourteen
—sitting-room, bedroom, and bath-room to each.
These are fitted up in various styles, not two alike,
but all in charming taste.   Much of the furniture
was specially designed for the rooms by distinguished French and German makers.   The royal
apartments at the Hotel Bristol and other caravan-
serais for crowned heads are like Tottenham Court
Road beside them.   The late King Alfonso had
heard so much about their beauty, and was so partial to Huelva otherwise, that in his last illness he
wished to go to the Hotel Colon.   Political reasons
required another selection to be made, but Huelva
expects that his son will, at no distant date, carry
out his unfulfilled wish.

The State apartments open on the garden behind,
through a large marble-paved hall.   This garden,
which is beautifully laid out in shrubberies, flower-
plots, fountains, and shady walks, is enclosed on
either side by a block containing the single bed-
rooms, and at the back are all the public rooms,
admirably arranged in a single building.   The
dining-room is a magnificent hall, which can also
be used as a ball-room, and on these occasions it
can accommodate nearly a thousand people.   The

ceiling is decorated with designs by Seville artists, and the fireplaces are of china, all specially made at the Royal Porcelain Factory in Meissen. A broad corridor runs round the hall, in which are the reading-room, billiard-room, card-rooms, &c. Fronting the whole of this block is a smooth paved terrace, where guests can drink their after-dinner coffee, gaze on the inconstant moon, and listen to the nightingales. Dost like the picture? I think you would if you saw it.

THE RABIDA.

FOR their next International Exposition the Americans have chosen a worthy subject and a memorable occasion. It will celebrate the four hundredth anniversary of the discovery of the New World, but the occasion should be no less honoured in the Old World, which has derived at least an equal share of advantage from it. If such a programme should be determined upon, I can suggest the most suitable place conceivable for carrying it out. The capitals of Europe would doubtless compete eagerly for the honour of offering it hospitality, but there is one insignificant and almost unknown spot in the south-east corner of Europe which has the best claim. Though identified with the greatest event in modern history, its name is little familiar even to the professed historian. It is a shrine which draws few pilgrims, though places of infinitely smaller interest are comparatively crowded with them. Not even the ubiquitous and irrepressible American tourist often finds his way to the Rabida. What, indeed, do nine-tenths of them know about the Rabida? The mention of it excites no emotion in their breasts, nor gives the slightest thrill to their imagination. Both the Old World and the New seem to have wholly forgotten the epoch-making event which happened at the Rabida nearly four centuries ago.

The most interesting chapter in Washington Irving's ' Life of Columbus ' opens thus: " About half a league from the little seaport of Palos de Moquer, in Andalusia, there stood, and continues to stand to the present day, an ancient convent of Franciscan friars, dedicated to Santa Maria de Rabida. One day, a stranger on foot, in humble guise, but of a distinguished air, accompanied by a small boy, stopped at the gate of the convent, and asked of the porter a little bread and water for his child. While receiving this humble refreshment, the prior of the convent, Juan Perez de Marchena, happening to pass by, was struck with the appearance of the stranger, and observing from his air and accent that he was a foreigner, entered into conversation with him, and soon learned the particulars of his story. That stranger was Columbus. He was on his way to the neighbouring town of Huelva, to seek his brother-in-law, who had married a sister of his deceased wife." When this fortunate encounter took place, Columbus was on the point of quitting Spain in disgust and disappointment, as he had quitted Portugal eight

E

years before. Ferdinand and Isabella had not
used him quite so meanly as John of Portugal did,
but after keeping him dangling at their heels all
through the Moorish war, they had broken with
him at last.

How different a history Spain might have had
but for the shrewd prior of the Rabida convent,
who at the eleventh hour arrested the departing
footsteps of Columbus! The great navigator might
have carried with him his idea of a western passage
to India to some more liberal Court, which would
have reaped the glory and the gain of realising it.
For aught we know, the next breeze of adventure
in his chequered life might have blown him toward
England, and found for him stauncher patrons in
the Tudors than in the twin houses of Arragon
and Castile. Luckily for Spain, the danger of let-
ting the unborn New World slip through her fingers
was averted. Prior Perez was not only a man of
intelligence, but he had influence at Court, having
once been private confessor to Queen Isabella.
He wrote a letter to her majesty, setting forth in
the most urgent terms the shame it would be to
Spain to cast away a chance, however small, of
achieving so noble an object as Columbus had in
view. This was sent to her by the hand of
Sebastian Rodriguez, a trusty pilot of Lepe, who
had become a keen convert to Columbus's scheme.
The womanly sympathy and the royal ambition
of Isabella were so effectually stirred by this
appeal that she returned an encouraging reply.

The prior was summoned to Court to confer with her further; and eventually her enthusiasm was so kindled that the objections of cold-hearted and envious courtiers were put down with the proud declaration: "I undertake the enterprise for my own crown of Castile, and will pledge my jewels to raise the necessary funds."

After all the royal jewels had not to be called on to finance the expedition. The cautious Ferdinand, though sceptical about the scheme, allowed seventeen thousand florins to be advanced from his treasury toward the expenses of it. Moreover, he took care to get repaid out of the first gold brought from the New World, which he employed in gilding the ceilings of his palace at Saragossa. Columbus himself had to find one-eighth of the required capital, which he raised among his new friends at the Rabida.

Their majesties Ferdinand and Isabella, if not strong in coin, could render valuable assistance in other shapes. They spared not royal decrees calling on their subjects for contributions in kind. The little seaport of Palos was already under obligation to provide annually two armed vessels, and these were for the current year assigned to the expedition. The Pinzons, a leading family in Palos, fitted out, at their own cost, a third vessel, the best in the little fleet. Two of the brothers also joined the expedition, and used all their local influence in recruiting men for it. The next public incident in the drama I borrow again from the graphic pages of Washington Irving : " The squadron being ready to put to sea, Columbus, impressed with the solemnity of his undertaking, confessed himself to the Prior Juan Perez, and partook of the sacrament of the Communion. His example was followed by his officers and crew, and they entered upon their enterprise full of awe and the most devout and affecting ceremonials, committing themselves to the especial guidance and protection of Heaven."

Now we come to the most graphic scene of all— the sad assembly on the sandy slope of the Rabida which bids God-speed to the explorers who were going forth, with their lives in their hands, to traverse unknown and possibly boundless seas. "It was," says Irving, "on the 3d August 1492, early in the morning, that Columbus set sail from the bar of Saltis, a small island formed by the arms of the Odiel, in front of the town of Huelva, steering in a south-westerly direction for the Canary Islands, whence it was his intention to strike due west." It is matter of history how the little fleet went straight ahead in its westward course until Columbus descried a light shining at a great distance. They made for it, and at dawn on the 12th October they found themselves anchored beside a level island several leagues in extent, and clothed from end to end with fruit-trees, as if it were one vast orchard. They took possession of it in the names of Ferdinand and Isabella, and called it San Salvador. It was one

of the Bahamas, the same to which English sailors
have given the much less poetic name of Cat Island. After going as far as Cuba, which he mis-
took for the mainland of Asia, perhaps the fabled
Cathay itself, Columbus returned by way of Hayti.
He had a very rough passage home, and anchored
on the 4th March 1493 off Cintra, at the mouth
of the Tagus.

In the hour of his triumph he did not forget the
humble port which had so befriended him in ad-
versity. As soon as he had paid his respects to
King John of Portugal he sailed again in his crazy
bark, the Nina, for his starting-place of seven and
a half months ago. On the 15th March he arrived
safely at the bar of Saltis, and at mid-day he
entered the little harbour of Palos. What spot
in Europe or in the world can match historical
incidents like these? What more worthy of grateful homage, or more likely to interest the intelligent pilgrim? When the Americans are celebrat-
ing the birth of their continent, they will commit
a grievous sin if they ignore the lonely convent of
the Rabida, or the little fishing village which now
represents the historical harbour of Palos.

THE STORY OF THE RIO TINTO.

IF Rio Tinto shares were suddenly to disappear from the official list there would be lamentation in the foreign market. Nevertheless, only twenty years ago the name would have had no meaning whatever to the most intelligent and wide-awake of foreign jobbers. It would have awakened no pleasant associations, or, indeed, associations of any kind, in Throgmorton Street. As the name of a small river in the south of Spain, it was quite outside the limits of financial geography. To-day it represents one of the greatest mineral properties ever known in history, and has been the subject of the wildest gamble in modern speculation. How in the course of half a generation it reached that proud eminence, is a fine example of the uncertainties of the mining lottery. The whole group of mines now known as Spanish copper mines—though one of them is, in fact, situated in Portugal —has had a romantic history, and most romantic of all is the Rio Tinto's.

Napoleon III.'s *coup d'état*, it will be remembered, set free many Frenchmen of anti-Bonapartist views to explore other countries. While many of them honoured us with their society in Leicester Square, and were content to earn a moderate, if precarious, livelihood as teachers of their own language, others of a more adventurous turn directed their attention to the South. Spain commended itself to them as an unexploited country, where finance and republicanism might be combined. They had heard of its mineral wealth, and though their knowledge of mining was shadowy, they had, like true Frenchmen, faith in themselves. They clubbed together a few thousand francs, and sent on a deputation in advance to survey the land. The deputies found their way to the province of Huelva, the most southern province of Spain, and then possessing but two claims to distinction : one, that it had fitted out the first expedition of Columbus to America ; and the other, that it was rich in old Roman mines, including, according to tradition, the Tharsis of Scripture.

So the French pioneers came down to Huelva, where lay the potentialities of growing rich beyond the dreams of avarice, as Dr Johnson used to say. They came to the Rio Tinto mine, which was then in charge of two Spanish engineers on behalf of the Government. The Spaniards were hospitable, showing them over all the property as it then was, and initiating them into the secrets of prospecting. Armed with the knowledge they had thus picked up, the Frenchmen explored the surrounding hills, and examined carefully all the old workings of which local tradition had preserved any account. They stumbled on the Tharsis, in an adjoining valley to the Tinto; and away to the west, beyond the Portuguese frontier, they found the once famous San Domingo mine, which became afterwards the Mason and Barry. Of those they preferred the middle deposit—a very great mistake for themselves, as it turned out. A lease of it was obtained with little difficulty from the Spanish Government, and a French society was formed to work it. Hence the Tharsis Company, the oldest of the so-called Spanish copper mines. The actual working of the property fell, however, into the hands of Scotsmen, who formed a company of their own in Glasgow, and crowded out the Parisians. Since then the Tharsis has been a Glasgow institution, as absolutely parochial and strictly private as St Rollox itself. It has no history beyond what Sir Charles Tennant and his cronies consider to be good for it—and themselves.

The Frenchmen having thus narrowly missed Rio Tinto, the Germans had a shot at it next, and it did not slip through their fingers. Spain was then, as it is still, the happy hunting-ground of exploiters of all nations. When the great German exodus began during the American civil war, thousands of young Teutons came over to London to learn the English art of money-making, in which so many of them have since beaten their masters.

Goschens, Huths, Murrietas, and all the principal foreign houses, were inundated with recruits ready to go anywhere and do anything in the way of honest business. Most of them had several languages at their finger-ends, and when an opening occurred at the River Plate or in the Philippine Islands, they were equally fit for it. One of these irrepressible young Germans, Wilhelm Sundheim, had come from Hesse Darmstadt with an introduction to Frederick Huth & Company—then, as now, the heads of a world-wide business. At their recommendation he went to the south of Spain, and broke ground in Seville, where he met with several compatriots, among others Mr Doetsch, now the managing director of Rio Tinto. Through an engineer who used to come up to Seville from Huelva, then a small fishing village, where there is now a population of over 20,000 souls, he heard that a good business was to be done in buying manganese ore from the small mines in the neighbourhood and shipping it to England.

Mr Sundheim promptly migrated to Huelva, and became a manganese merchant and shipper, first in partnership with a friend who went from London to join him, and afterwards with Mr Doetsch, who has been his associate in a great variety of undertakings, radiating from their original manganese agency. They have built railways, opened up mines, laid out vineyards, developed marble quarries, and turned their busy hands to everything they found an opening for. The

Huelva of to-day is their creation, and that of the Rio Tinto Company. To them it owes its hotel—the largest and finest south of Madrid—its harbour improvements, its railway communication with the North, but, above all, its pre-eminence as the greatest mineral shipping port in Europe.

It was through another German that they came to know about the Rio Tinto. Mr Blum, a trained mining-engineer and mineralogist, had been for several years prospecting all over Spain when Mr Sundheim came to Huelva. He had, at last, settled down near the Tharsis mine, watching with great interest the progress of the new French Company. From time to time he visited the Rio Tinto, which was being spasmodically and, as a rule, unprofitably worked by the Spanish Government. He saw that, though it did not pay, it was opening out a splendid mine, and that valuable information he communicated to his friends Sundheim and Doetsch. They on their side kept a sharp look-out for financial opportunities, which were not long in coming. The Spanish Government was carrying on a desperate struggle for life amid the bankruptcy and anarchy into which it had been plunged by the recent Carlist war. It could only pay its way by realising all the loose property of the State convertible into coin. When a hint was given it that a purchaser might be found for the Rio Tinto copper mines, it rose to the bait eagerly. A bill, virtually drafted by Messrs Sundheim and Doetsch, and piloted through the

Cortes by a provincial deputy of Huelva, empowered it to have the mines valued and put up for sale by public auction. This was done, and they were knocked down for nearly four millions sterling to a syndicate of London and Bremen capitalists, with Messrs Matheson & Co. at its head.

RIO TINTO UNDER THE SWEDES.

NEXT to agriculture, mining is the oldest industry in the world, and the one which has had most influence on human progress. In historic times, wherever a country has enjoyed exceptional prosperity, mining is the most probable cause. It must have " struck " something, whether iron, copper, tin, or gold. Cornish tin attracted Phœnician. and Roman adventurers, who would never have been tempted by the finest of Devonshire pastures, or the heaviest wheat-crop in Sussex. Long before the Christian era, the Iberian Peninsula was to Rome what Mexico, and Peru afterwards, became to Spain herself—an El Dorado. The old mines have to tell their own story, for otherwise there is not much record of them. In very few cases does any trace survive of how the Romans actually mined. There must have been many contemporary chronicles; and the burning of the Alexandrian Library is perhaps responsible for this, as for so many other literary losses which cannot be redeemed. At all events, the Roman age of mining is, so far as documents go, virtually a blank. A few incidental allusions to it have been found on tablets, and the remains of what is supposed to have been a book of mining regulations were unearthed some time ago in Portugal. Beyond that there is no evidence, save the workings themselves and the relics discovered in them.

All through the Sierra Morena, extending from Seville to the Portuguese frontier, the Roman miners have left their mark. Wherever they had an important camp, a copper or a silver mine is sure not to have been far off. Many of these have been rediscovered, and many more await resurrection, which they are likely to have in the next few years. Local traditions gathered round the chief of them, and preserved their memory through the long night of the Middle Ages. Rio Tinto, Tharsis, and San Domingo, the three great Peninsular mines of our own time, were probably as famous two thousand years ago as they are now. They may have been the chief mining centres of the Romans in Southern Spain. It is certain that they were worked in the reigns of the Emperors Nerva and Honorius, and all through the later Empire. The Moors, of course, would let them go down, for the Koran favours agriculture as against mining. While Moorish industry and the art of irrigation were turning the plains of Andalusia into a garden, the Sierra Morena, teeming everywhere with mineral wealth, relapsed into a desert.

Only after the expulsion of the Moors did mining revive in Southern Spain, and then it recovered but slowly ; for the best thoughts of Spain were directed to the New World. A new Golconda was hunted for in the West, by men who were leaving far richer treasures behind them untouched and uncared for. It was not till the middle of the sixteenth century that the lost mines of the Old World were again inquired for, and still it was not by the Spaniards themselves, but by foreigners. The Swedes were the miners of that day, and their enterprise or cupidity carried them all over Europe. Some of them got as far south as Huelva, drawn, perhaps, by the legend that there was to be found the Tharsis of the Bible. There is reason to believe that the whole district from San Domingo to Rio Tinto bore the generic name of Tharsis.

It is a strange example of the irony of history, that when Columbus sailed on his first voyage to America, he left behind him, within fifty or sixty miles of the fishing port he sailed from, mineral deposits which were destined to produce a more famous mine of its kind than has yet been discovered across the Atlantic. The dark waters of the Rio Tinto, on which his pioneer ships floated out into the unknown ocean, owe their colour to a mountain of copper which has yielded almost as many solid millions of money as have been got out of the Comstock lode, or the Calumet and

Hecla. The age of Columbus was an age of navigators and adventurers. The miner was still in his infancy, and the mining prospecter had not yet been born. The art of exploring the bowels of the earth, for which there was ample scope at home, had to be learned in Mexico, and thence had to be brought back to Europe. It was the dazzling example of Potosi which first started a serious search for mining prizes in Europe. And even then the stimulus operated slowly and irregularly. Enlightened sovereigns as Ferdinand and Isabella were in many respects, their keen vision never penetrated below the surface of the earth on which they played so stormy a part. There is no trace of mining ever having engaged their attention ; and little mention of mining operations is to be found in their royal archives.

The first distinct allusion to the mineral deposits of Southern Spain occurs only about the middle of the sixteenth century. It is a State paper belonging to the reign of Charles V., and bears date 15th August 1556. Its formal title is — "Report on the Mines of Zalamea la Vieja and those of Rio Tinto — Ministry of Public Works, No. 28." This curious document was unearthed in 1831 by Toma Gonzalez during his investigation of the historical antiquities of Zalamea, which is to Spain what Cornwall is to England—the cradle of its mining industry. Like sixteenth century history in general, it is freely compounded of fable and romance, with a very small

percentage of fact. The waters of the Rio Tinto
are said to be so black as to serve very well for ink,
and so pungent that any metal plunged into them
gets melted in a few days. So enormous are the
masses of ore, that "they look like great hills and
mountains." This seductive picture seems not to
have been painted altogether in vain. It excited
the cupidity of Don Alvaro Alonzo de Garfias, who
applied for a licence to work the mines of Zalamea
and Rio Tinto. Apparently he obtained it, for a
royal warrant was issued in his favour; but what
he made of it, or what it made of him, there is no
record. Don Alvaro Alonzo de Garfias is but a
passing shadow on the first vestiges of Rio Tinto
history.

Such another shadow was Don Sebastian Vallejo,
who is referred to in 1680 as the then lessee of the
mines. At that early date the "precipitation" process was already in use, and Don Sebastian applied
it with more zeal then caution. Having failed to
guard himself against an over-supply of water,
one unlucky day he got washed out. According
to a royal warrant, issued from Aranguez in May
1695, his successor was Don Roque de Salas y
Ulloa. From the text of the warrant it may be
gathered that copper and various other metals
were being extracted from the waters of the Rio
Tinto by such rude methods as the science of the
day had attained. Another long blank occurs
here, and no further reference to Rio Tinto is dis-
coverable till 1719, when Don Nicholas Vaillant

submitted to the Spanish Government a proposal
to lease for thirty years " the mines of Guadalcanal,
Gazalla, Galaroso, Rio Tinto, and Aracena." The
specification of five different groups of mines sug-
gests that in the interval since 1680 some successful prospecting had been done. The Sierra Morena,
and its offshoots in Estramadura, had been system-
atically explored with considerable results.

To this day Don Vaillant's five mines represent
the principal mining districts in Southern Spain,
and some of them still await thorough development. Galaroso, for instance, has only of late
been taken energetically in hand. A Rio Tinto
syndicate, directed by Messrs Doetsch & Sundheim, are now prosecuting, with all the appliances
of modern science, the gigantic work which Don
Vaillant must have found a great deal too much
for him at the beginning of the eighteenth century.
His footsteps have been lost on the sands of time,
and nothing is known of him now beyond the bare
fact that, on the 6th June 1719, his scheme was
provisionally approved by the *Consejo de Hacienda*
(Ministry of Public Works). It went no further,
however. Either from lack of capital, or through
excess of red tape in the Public Works Department,
no result was reached till five years later, when a
more notable man came on the scene. Lieberto
Wolters, a Swede, and apparently the first practical miner who had yet touched the Rio Tinto,
entered into negotiations with the Government on
the basis of Don Vaillant's still-born proposal. A

F

notable man in many ways, he cut a figure in
Spanish finance as well as in mining. He had
already been in business relations with the Court,
and evidently knew how to manipulate it, for the
concession he obtained in 1725 reads as if it had
been very liberal.

A Spanish admiral, Manuel de Velasco, had
wrecked part of his fleet at Vigo, and Don Wolters
took a contract for salvage, which probably paid
him pretty well. When Don Nicholas Vaillant
failed to carry through his scheme for leasing the
five mines, Wolters offered to proceed with it on
somewhat different conditions. In June 1725 a
royal decree was signed granting him a lease for
thirty years, after which all his buildings, plant,
and other assets, with the exception of ore or
metal on hand, were to revert to the Crown. An
assessor was to be appointed by the Crown to
protect its rights, and to levy a royalty on the
produce of the mines at the rate of one-thirtieth,
which afterwards became the standard mining
royalty in Spain. The accounts between Don
Wolters and the Government got into such hopeless confusion, that they have not been cleared up,
I believe, to this day ; and it was partly to get rid
once and for all of the claims of his heirs, that
an absolute sale was made of the Rio Tinto sixteen
years ago.

This lease is full of the most interesting historical reminiscences. It provides that foreign labourers working at the mines shall not be molested

on account of their religion, if they keep it to themselves, but they are not to exercise it in public. Flemings were at that time being imported in large numbers from the Low Countries, and this guarantee of rel'gious liberty seems to have been regularly given to them, though not always scrupulously observed, it may be. An important colony of them was established at Guadalajara for cloth-weaving, and traces of it exist still. The lessee is to have the right to cut wood for charcoal all over the mountains within a certain radius of the mines—an indication that the mountains were much better timbered then than they are now. One would go a long way now from Rio Tinto before he found either a bush or a blade of grass. But the Spanish Government was more favourable to mining enterprise then than it seems to be to-day. It recognised the fact that mining and agriculture could not live happily together, and should not try to. A specified area round the mines was given over to Don Lieberto Wolters, and trespassing on it was absolutely forbidden. The difficulty about calcination, which is now being made a political stalking-horse at Madrid, could not possibly have arisen then, for Don Lieberto Wolters was made monarch of all he surveyed from the blood-red ridge of the Cerro Salamon. Still another historical incident worth noting in the lease of 1725, is an allusion to the Almaden quicksilver mines, proving them to have been already in active operation. One of the many privileges stipulated for by the cautious Don Wolters, was that he should get from Almaden all the salt and saltpetre he required at the same price as was charged to the Royal Hacienda, but that for the *azogue* (quicksilver) he should pay 400 reals a quintal. Very nice business that must have been for the Almaden.

Don Lieberto Wolters was not only a projector, but he anticipated some of the modern devices of joint-stock finance. No sooner had he secured the five mines, than he invited the public to club together their ducats and share his prize with him. As a company promoter he was in no important respect far behind his successors of to-day. He had graduated even in the mysteries of underwriting and vendors' shares. His scheme, which he published at Madrid in September 1725, under the quaint name of a 'Manifesto,' formed a twenty-five page pamphlet, very clearly written, and well digested throughout. A company, or rather a cost-book venture on the Cornish model, was to be constituted, with a capital of 100,000 doubloons, in 2000 shares of 50 doubloons each. The equivalent of a doubloon being an ounce of gold, this meant in sterling about £375,000, of which Don Lieberto claimed for himself as founder 700 shares, or fully a third of the capital, and the other 1300 shares were thrown open to subscription. Not a single bait was omitted which financial science has learned to dress its hook with. Payment by easy instalments was arranged for, only 10 doub-

loons per share being asked cash down ; 10 more
were to be paid in March 1726, six months afterwards, and the rest " as required."

What sort of an allotment Don Lieberto made
is, unfortunately, no longer ascertainable, but cas-
ual allusions in the later history of the company
indicate that it had some distinguished shareholders. The Marquis de la Paz became first
President of the Council, and dukes and grandees
took a lively part in its consultations. Don
Lieberto may have allowed them to " underwrite
a bit," or possibly the 700 shares which he reserved as founder did not all remain with him.
There may have been secret contracts, under which
they had to "go round." From the days of the
Phœnicians it has always been much easier to
get experience than dividends out of a new mine.
So Don Lieberto and his shareholders found it.
They had so few facts and so many ideas to go
upon, that they were soon all by the ears. Don
Lieberto's leisure time was entirely absorbed by
a hot paper war with a dissentient party in the
Council, headed by the Marquis de Villadorrias.
Repeatedly the king had to interfere and impose
modifications of the lease, to please the faction
which happened at the moment to have the upper
hand. In the end, Don Lieberto's position in the
undertaking became considerably weakened, and
things were not prospering with him when he
died, suddenly, at the mines in June 1727.

With characteristic forethought he had pro-

vided a successor in his nephew, Samuel Tiquet,
like himself a Swede. He was a practical miner,
who had gained considerable credit and experience
in his own country, and the result justified his
selection as new manager. He pulled the company round some stiff corners, one of them with
an English peeress, who got mixed up in a strange
way with Rio Tinto. The Earl of Powis of that
day, being a keen Roman Catholic and a Jacobite,
found it more convenient to live in Spain than in
England. After his death his widow remained in
Spain, or, at all events, invested money in the
country. Among other speculations she came to
the help of Samuel Tiquet when he was hard-up,
and advanced him large sums for opening up the
mines. At various times between 1740 and 1742
he gave her *cedulas* or acknowledgments of in-
debtedness, on which, failing repayment, she fore-
closed. In 1742 she obtained actual possession of
the mines, and proceeded at once to demolish the
vitriol and copperas works. Why, it is impossible
to guess, unless on the general principle that she
was a woman. But Samuel Tiquet got the best
of her after all. As the result of a long and
costly suit before the Cortes, the company was
reinstated in its property, but not released from its
difficulties.

In 1746 the lease was prolonged for thirty years,
which, had there been no further slips between the
cup and the lip, would have carried on Samuel
Tiquet to 1776; but many things happened in the

interval. On 14th September 1747 the share-holders of the " Mining Company of Rio Tinto and Aracena," as it was now called, held a meeting at Seville. It was a rough meeting, and not the first of that sort by any means. The vitriol and cop-peras works, which the irate Countess of Powis had pulled down, must be rebuilt; but who was to find the money? Samuel Tiquet, like his uncle, was an ingenious schemer, and could always pro-duce a plan when wanted. He now submitted calculations showing that, for a sum of 153,800 reals, works could be built which would increase the output of vitriol and copperas from 368 reals to over 2000 reals a-day. A call of 25 doubloons per share would provide the 153,800 reals, and he proposed to have it made forthwith. But there were various other meetings of shareholders at Seville before the question was decided, and the exact outcome of it is not clear. Tiquet appears to have struggled on in a very hand-to-mouth fashion, selling shares when he could, borrowing from whoever would lend to him, and running into debt with whoever would trust him. By this time the 700 founder's shares reserved by Don Lieberto Wolters had been nearly all melted down. About three-quarters of a million reals had been realised from them and put in the mine, which now had at debit of its capital account 1,707,000 reals, equal to nearly £14,000.

Tiquet died in 1758, and the last years of his life were a close-handed fight with creditors, who

bore down on him from all quarters. Among the
papers he left behind him, and which were carefully preserved, are an inventory of the property
in the mine, and a memorandum of the yearly
output from 1747 to 1758—the first period of real
production it had. It started with 24 *arrobas* (25
lb. each, or, roughly speaking, a quarter of a cwt.)
Imagine the Rio Tinto when it could produce only
600 lb. of copper in twelve months! From 1747
there was a gradual increase to 536 *arrobas* in
1752, and then a jump to 1561 *arrobas* in the following year. In 1756 the production exceeded
3000 *arrobas*, but in 1758, Tiquet's last year, it fell
again to little better than 2000 *arrobas*. The
standard price of copper then was 4½ reals, or
11¼d. per lb., and rarely did it drop to 4¼ reals.
There was nothing to complain of on the score of
price, though at the same time it was not exor-
bitant. £105 per ton, the equivalent of 4½ reals
per lb., would have satisfied even the Copper Syndicate, and just now the copper trade is fairly happy
with half as much.

Tiquet, either through holding a majority of the
shares, or by special contract, had the right to
appoint his successor. He named his country-
man and friend Francesco Tomas Sanz, and then
another troubled reign began. Sanz, though ad-
ministrator, could not administer without the co-
operation of various colleagues, whose interests
and ideas were different from his. An ingeniously
managed *junta* of officials tied each other's hands,

and devoted their whole energy to squabbling.
The memorials they fired at each other through
the Council of Commerce, Money, and Mines
would soon have driven any but Spanish Ministers angry; but Spanish officials love paper war
next to a bull-fight. They let the campaign go
on for years until the term of the Wolters concession approached. Then the Government stepped
in, and in terms of the lease took possession, turning out administrators, assessors, superintendents,
shareholders, and all together. Thus violently
ended the Swedish *régime* in Rio Tinto, which laid
in apparent disaster the foundations of a magnificent success. To this day the descendants of
Wolters and Tiquet urge on the Spanish Government their claims to compensation for having been
expropriated from the Rio Tinto a hundred and
ten years ago. Like some other historical law-
suits, it makes very slow progress.

THE
ANGLO-GERMAN RIO TINTO.

IN 1777 a new era began in the history of Rio Tinto. The Spanish Government then took up the mine, not so much, perhaps, for making profit out of it as to obtain an easy supply of currency. The working was of the very roughest kind, the ore having been hauled out of the mine by donkeys, the calcining operations having been all done by hand, and the precipitate having been sent down on donkeys or mules to Seville. It was refined at the Mint, and, presumably, the bulk of the metal obtained was minted forthwith. The anarchy into which Spain was plunged by the French invasion and the subsequent campaigns of the Duke of Wellington, put an end even to these very limited operations. From 1809 to 1829, a period of fully twenty years, Rio Tinto was abandoned. A lease of it was then given to a Frenchman, Gaspar Remise, who held it at an annual rent down to 1849. The Spanish Government now resumed possession, and began to develop the property with some spirit. Numerous borings were made along the supposed line of the lode, all of which were minutely shown on the official plans on which the sale was made to the present owners in 1872.

These test shafts and borings turned out, as a rule, rather wide of the mark, and have not been closely verified by actual experience. They showed three fine broad lodes running parallel with each other, which in the original maps of the company were distinguished as the South, the Middle, and the North lodes. The two last were run into each other at both ends, and had a much greater length given them than they were really entitled to ; in fact, they were fitted nicely into the available space, and if paying ore were to be found all through their length, the Rio Tinto would still be in its infancy when the last trump gave the final signal to stop work. On the other hand, the so-called south lode, now known to be the main lode, has turned out a great deal better than it shows on the Spanish plans. They extend it to the east, where it has not yet been discovered, and they ignore that magnificent continuation westward, the San Dionysio lode, which may turn out to be the kernel of the deposit.

Of course the calculations of the Spanish engineers were taken *cum grano* by their English and German colleagues. Mr Forbes virtually put aside the two upper lodes altogether, and dealt only with that portion of the south or main lode which had been actually opened. He took a section of it, 400 mètres (1200 ft.) long, and, assuming that the mineral continued the same size and quality down to 85 mètres as it was then at the 65 mètre level, he calculated that there would be 11,700,000 tons of ore to get out. Very much more has already been got, though not from that particular spot. At the present rate of production, say, 1,400,000 tons per annum, the 11,700,000 tons anticipated by Mr Forbes would be only eight years' supply. It may with greater confidence be predicted to-day that there is eighty years' supply in the mine, than in 1872 it could be predicted that it would last eight years. What the property was bought on is now a mere fragment of its proved mineral contents. Rio Tinto is one of the rare mines which the prospectus-monger has been unable to make a fool of. Figure up as wildly as he pleased, he would still be far short of the reality.

It was in 1872 that the Rio Tinto mine passed out of the hands of the Spanish Government into those of the London Bremen Syndicate, who risked nearly four millions sterling in it to start with, and had put nearly as much again into it before they had it in full operation. There is no larger venture of its kind on record, or one which has turned out so brilliantly. Its pioneers were not plungers. They played for a big stake, but they played very cautiously all the same. The property was three different times reported on by competent men before it was offered to the public, who nevertheless

had so little faith in it at first as to sell many of
their original £10 shares for thirty shillings apiece.
Within three years they were buying back again at
over £30 apiece.   The first expert who went over
the property was the Mr Blum already referred to.
He became afterwards the mining manager of the
syndicate, and for a time held a similar position
under the company; but differences of opinion
with his English colleagues as to the most profitable method of developing the mine caused him to
throw up his appointment.   He returned to his
original business of mining prospecter, and is still
busy among the hillsides of the Sierra Morena
looking out for new Rio Tintos.   I hope he may
find one, and be more fortunate over it than he
was with the original.   On the whole, he had more
of the hard knocks and less of the consoling
success than he might have fairly expected at Rio
Tinto.   Disputes and differences of opinion there
were bound to be at the outset of such a novel and
gigantic undertaking, but events have in most cases
justified the hard-headed, rough-spoken Blum.
That much should be recorded to his credit, and
will be readily admitted by those who differed from
him years ago.

After getting all the local information which Mr
Blum could supply, the syndicate sent down one of
the most eminent geologists of the day, Professor
Roemer, of Breslau University, to inspect the mine.
He made a very elaborate and, on the whole, favour-
able report, which decided the syndicate to pur-

chase. When, subsequently, the company was brought out, Messrs Matheson sent down the best man they could get hold of, Mr David Forbes, to make a second inspection. He was on the ground from the middle of March to the 9th April 1873, and examined everything thoroughly under the guidance of Mr Blum and the Spanish Government engineers. His confidential report, a proof of which I have read with great interest, gives a historical account of the property from the time of the Romans, describes how it had been worked by the Spaniards, and concludes with a scheme for increasing the output to what Mr Forbes evidently considered the enormous output of *two thousand tons per annum.* Had he been told that before the Rio Tinto Company was out of its teens it would be producing *over twenty thousand tons of copper per annum,* Mr Forbes might not have found it in his heart thus to swamp the copper market.

His prophetic soul would have been still more aghast had he foreseen the effect of Rio Tinto on the price of copper. His calculations were made on the basis of £62, 8s. per ton, the average cost of production by the Spaniards in 1869. This he thought left a safe margin of £30 per ton profit! And within the past twelve months we have seen copper offered for sale in East India Avenue at £35 per ton, or only a few pounds above what in 1873 the manufacturer expected to get out of it as his own share. Very few mines in the world can afford to sell copper at £35 per ton, and it has

been doubted if even the Rio Tinto could live at
such a figure. The management have hitherto
been reticent on that subject, and rightly so for
various reasons. It might be inexpedient to show
one's hand too much to competitors, but a better
reason is that the conditions which determine cost
of production in Rio Tinto are too diverse and
variable to be easily explained. The chairman
himself could not at a given date say, " Copper is
costing us so much per ton all round." The mines
produce not one article but half-a-dozen, all coming
originally from the same lode, but going through
different sets of processes, incurring special charges,
and ending at different destinations. While there
are expenses common to all, such as " establishment " and " removal of over-burden," each product
has some peculiar to itself.

Ore shipped to England would not seem to
require a great deal of book-keeping, but it does.
First, it is chargeable with its quota of establishment and over-burden expenses ; next with actual
cost of mining and handling at the mine ; lastly,
with transport and selling expenses in this country.
The final result, whatever it may be, is subject,
on the other hand, to deductions and allowances.
Sulphur as well as copper being obtained from the
ore, must bear its share of costs. Thus in its very
simplest form the cost of producing copper at a
mine like Rio Tinto is a rather complex problem.
For the calcined ores quite another set of accounts
has to be kept. They are chargeable with estab-

lishment and "over-burden" as before, next with
their own particular cost of extraction, then with
calcining, washing, precipitating—a very elaborate
process—transport, and last of all, with refining in
this country. *Per contra*, they have to be credited
with the value of the metal left in the ore after the
first washing, and which may not be fully recovered
for years after. This opens up a new and very
interesting account. The residuum of the calcined
ores goes along with the "smalls" to grass, as it
were ; it is spread out in heaps, measuring millions
of tons, which, as they decompose, have water
filtered through them to wash out the copper.
The water is then led into reservoirs and precipi-
tated—a very ingenious method of treating poor
ores at practically no expense.

A very small proportion of Rio Tinto ore—about
five per cent—is rich enough to be worth smelting
on the spot. It is only put through the first stage,
moreover, and then sent home as *regulus* or *matte*.
It has to be charged with the quota of establishment and "over-burden," its own cost of extraction
and dressing, and finally, with cost of smelting and
shipment. It makes the fifth product of the Rio
Tinto mines of which distinct account has to be
kept—the others being copper from shipped ores,
sulphur from ditto, copper from calcined ores after
first washing, copper from subsequent washings,
and from smalls. It may be readily perceived
that cost of production under so many different
circumstances must vary widely. There can be no

average in the proper sense of the word, for each class has its own cost continually varying and affecting the general average differently as its relative amount may be large or small. In a year when there is more calcined ore and less shipped ore, the cost of production per ton overhead will be higher than when there is less ore calcined and more shipped.

Strange to say, the very poorest stuff costs least to realise. "Smalls" and calcined residue go into the washing-heaps at an average cost of £6 per ton for actual outlay, but at £15 per ton including their proportion of establishment and "overburden." A few pounds per ton additional will cover the expense of their further treatment. Hence we have the paradox that the poorest kind of ore known yields the cheapest copper. This particular product the Rio Tinto Company can, I have little doubt, put in the market for under £20 per ton. The metal obtained from calcining and first washing should not be much more expensive, neither should the ore shipped after being credited with the sulphur it yields. I have purposely avoided this delicate subject both with the company's manager and agents here, preferring the general estimate made on my own responsibility to any official information which might be compromising. But it may be given as the local opinion of the district that Rio Tinto is now producing copper for less than £30 per ton, and to me the statement is quite credible.

G

RIO TINTO ABOVE GROUND.

IN these confusing altitudes I almost forget whether there be seven wonders of the world and ten commandments, or seven commandments and ten wonders of the world, but whichever it is, Rio Tinto comes next. There can be no possible mistake about Rio Tinto. No need in its case to caution the public against spurious imitations, or to announce that nothing is genuine without this label on the box. Creation has given us only one Vesuvius, one Niagara Falls, one Rio Tinto. That is not a very graphic or intelligible description, I admit; but who could describe such a scene. It is a world by itself, shut in among the desolate, sun-scorched mountains of the Sierra Morena. To do justice to so weird and supernatural a landscape, it should be peopled by hobgoblins working in subterranean smithies, eating brimstone with long spoons, and slaking their thirst with the blood-red waters of the Tinto river. If Mr Irving were to come and have a look at it, he would reluctantly confess that his Walpurgis Nacht in "Faust" was tame in comparison. The demoniac grandeur of the Rio Tinto is infinitely greater than could be reproduced even on the Lyceum stage, and, moreover, it is all real.

Who then can be expected to describe it? Dante might have done so had he been allowed a lifetime to the task ; but, following the example of modern poet-laureates, his rate per line would have been appalling—too much, perhaps, even for "*the Rialto*" treasury. Present readers must be satisfied with a more prosaic and modestly-drawn picture. Imagine, then, an area of nearly five thousand acres, or eight square miles—as large, say, as London north of Euston Road. It is covered from end to end with masses of red and grey earth, looking like gigantic ash-heaps. A few of these are the natural hill-tops, which it has not been thought worth while to remove ; but most of them are artificial mounds formed during the operations of the mine. That towering mass of broken slate and granite in the distance was made by the Romans, whose implements and domestic utensils are found in it to the present day. That high embankment of blood-red clay and porphyry, with two lines of railway running along the top of it, is "over-burden" or barren ground removed from the "open cast." It represents millions of tons weight, and has been carried miles away from where nature placed it. In the hollow below there is as much slag or cinder from the blast-furnaces as would pave all London, and it is but a fraction of what the furnaces have turned out. Every year thousands of tons of it are put on the railway as ballast, and wherever a chance occurs it is made away with ; but still it goes on growing.

Rio Tinto was wild and desolate enough when the copper miners laid hold of it ; but that was grace and beauty compared with what it is now. Pluto himself, lurid as his fancy is supposed to be, could not have conceived the idea of such a scorched, scarified, and grimy wilderness as it has since become. It is pandemonium painted red and set out to roast in a blazing sun. All around, the sun-baked earth, the hard grey slate, and the black cinder rise in an amphitheatre of mounds and terraces. Fantastic in shape and in shape-lessness, they look like the world on the eve of creation, "without form, and void." But most of them have, in fact, been carefully planned. A great deal of thinking has been bestowed on them, and when we have opportunity to examine them closely it will appear that, outcast as they look, they are still essential parts of the working of the mine. The terraces are traversed by nearly 60 miles of railway, on which more than 30 locomotives and 750 waggons are running daily. From one end of the workings to the other is a journey by rail of seven or eight miles, curving in and out of hollows, crossing points, running up one slope and down another, and your engine all the while shrieking to signalmen at every few hundred yards. Walking is out of the question in such a country. Short journeys the superintendents do on horseback, but for long ones they have to take the rail. When they wish to look round, instead of calling a hansom, they send for an engine and car. It takes them quickly over the ground, and gives them a good elevation to see from.

In future, when I hear Macbeth talking about a "blasted heath," I shall have to tell him confidentially that he knows nothing at all about it. Not having been at Rio Tinto, he can have very little notion of the real thing. His "blasted heath" was merely a dramatic background to Birnam Wood, and doubtless it nowadays affords very good grouse-shooting. But Rio Tinto has no alleviations like these. It is pandemonium without any weaknesses or the slightest signs of repentance. Not a blade of grass is to be seen for miles around. The nearest shrub of which there is any authentic record is about half a day's journey away in the Sierra. In the lower valley, red-capped oleanders flourish along the driest water-courses wherever there is a crevice in the flinty rock to get a footing in, but they have never tried it on at Rio Tinto. There the only verdure is the green phosphorescent film over the calcining heaps. It is a strong, but not very salubrious form of vegetation. The calcining heaps continue to be, in more senses than one, a burning question at Rio Tinto. They assert

themselves at an early period of one's visit to the
happy valley, and they continue more or less in
evidence to the end. First seen and last lost sight
of, they remain to memory dear.

Get up pretty early of a morning and look out
from your window across the plateau. In the
centre of it there will be a sulphurous mist hanging—not quite so villanously yellow as a London
fog, but bad enough. As the sun rises this gets
cleared away, and after eight or nine o'clock in the
morning it causes little trouble. But in the rainy
season and in dull weather it hangs longer, and if
the wind should blow it toward the houses, there
will be a day of penance. Unquestionably the
calcining heaps are no luxury, but it is not for the
people who live by them to complain of them.
Without the calciners there might be no Rio
Tinto, or, at least, it would have to be a much
smaller concern. . Legally, also, they have the best
of it. They were first in possession, and the
people came to them—not they to the people.
Calcining was very probably practised by the
Romans ages ago, and it certainly was by the
Spanish Government all the time that it worked
the mines. The calciners were specially mentioned as a valuable part of the property, and,
what is more, the process was affirmed to be perfectly healthy—salubrious rather than otherwise.
That it is not unhealthy is proved by the death-
rate of Rio Tinto being considerably lower than in
Madrid itself.

This Hades among the mountains supports a population of over 12,000 people, seven-eighths of whom are at work in the mines or on the railway. They live partly in the old Spanish town, which sleeps on as placidly as ever at the back of the central hill, and partly in villages specially built for them by the company at points most convenient for their work. Wherever there is a shaft or a furnace, or a set of precipitating tanks standing by itself, there is sure to be seen, perched on an adjoining knoll, a group of red-roofed, white-washed houses for the workmen. The old town itself is a straggling street, leading uphill to a square-roofed church, behind which is a neat, well-paved *plaza*, with seats all round it for the convenience of serenaders. About half a mile to the west, on the shoulder of another hill, is the English town—a double row of brick houses, evidently roomy, and said to be very comfortable. Immediately behind these is the chapel, a serviceable if not very ecclesiastical-looking building. It was the Rio Tinto pavilion at the Madrid Exhibition, and afterwards was dedicated to the Church. If a school for the English children of the place were to be combined with it, its usefulness, I am told, would be greatly increased. But that is a polemical subject considerably removed from copper.

RIO TINTO UNDERGROUND.

IF Rio Tinto above ground be appalling, underground it is magnificent. Human eye has never
before seen such a wide-spreading and apparently
endless mass of mineral as is there being laid open.
For aught we know, or are ever likely to know,
these mines have been worked for centuries, perhaps thousands of years. Millions of tons of stuff
have been taken out of them in our own time, and
who shall say how many more millions were raised
by the Phœnicians, the Romans, and their various
successors since the Christian era began? But the
surface of the deposit is hardly scratched as yet.
So far from showing any sign of exhaustion, there
is more ore in sight at this moment than can ever
have been before. Taken as a whole, the mine has
been opening out better in the past two years than
it ever did. Some workings have, of course, seen
their best; but for every old one wearing out there
is a new one of far greater promise coming into
operation. On the east side of the "open cast"

the main lode is narrowing, and may in a short time be lost; but to the west it is growing both in breadth and depth.

In the San Dionysio, cross-cuts of over four hundred feet have been made, and are still in mineral. A ten or twelve feet lode would delight the heart of a mining captain anywhere else, but when you go down into the Rio Tinto you must put on seven-league boots if you would get over the ground. The enormous surface becomes small when compared with the magnitude of the tunnels and galleries underground. Most of them are large enough for a full-sized locomotive to run in; and the main tunnel, which runs in direct from the Huelva Railway, follows the lode for a distance of over two miles. Branch tunnels fork off from it to the north lode and other parts of the mine, placing every important working in direct communication with the railway. It would be possible to lode ore in the mine and to discharge it into the steamer at Huelva without ever touching it again. As a matter of fact it has to be turned out on the sorting-floors to be sized and dressed. After that operation, however, the shipping ores have only one other handling to go through. They are loaded into trucks which run on to the company's pier at Huelva, where, as soon as they come alongside the shute, a bolt is drawn and a whole waggon-load at a time tumbles into the ship's hold.

I have referred to the Rio Tinto ground as being about as large as London north of Euston Road.

That illustration may be further utilised to indicate the bearings of the principal workings. Somewhere about Mother Redcap would be the famous
"open cast" or quarry, which hitherto has been
the mainstay of the mine, though later develop-
ments have reduced it to a secondary feature.
West of it the lode has been followed into what is
called the *contre mine ;* and still further west, about
as far, say, as St John's Wood, the San Dionysio
lode opens out—just now the most hopeful-looking
part of the property. The Cerro Colorado, a hill
out of the south face of which the "open cast" has
been scooped, has behind it—as it were at Hamp-
stead—a smaller hill through which the north lode
runs. It is the oldest part of the mine, but as yet
the least developed. The Romans worked it to a
certainty, for their spoil-heaps are still visible. In
the locality they are known as the *Escorias Romanos*,
and Roman remains of various kinds place their
origin beyond doubt. When taken over from the
Spaniards both this hill and the Cerro Colorado
were honeycombed with short shafts, from which
great quantities of ore had evidently been ab-
stracted. The theory is that, as only the better
ores could be worked by the Romans, they had to
hunt round for them, and consequently they preferred a lot of shallow sinkings to two or three
deep ones.

These old shafts are now fast disappearing. In
the "open cast" they have been completely cleared
away, and the lowest bench now being worked is

at least a couple of hundred feet below them. In
the north lode they will soon follow, for, on the
advice of its mining-engineers (Mr Osborne and
Mr Rich), the Board has decided to work it also on
the "open cast" system. At the time of my visit
a gang of labourers had begun to clear away the
"over-burden," which in this case means practically
the whole top of the hill. They begin by running
a deep cut into it, from which they make other
cuts, until sufficient room has been obtained for a
safe slope. The Roman shafts and the Spanish
borings have proved where the mineral is, and
further certainty has been got from the extensive
underground workings of the company itself. A
branch tunnel was years ago run out from the
original "open cast," and galleries were driven
from it into the mineral. These might easily be
worked as they are; but it was a question of
economy between them and making a fresh start
from the surface at the "open cast." When the
latter has been carried down, it will always be in
the option of the engineers to resume underground
working, if thought more advisable, or the two may
be carried on together.

In the same way it is a pending question at the
old "open cast" if that system should not be abandoned in favour of regular sinking. An inclined
shaft has already been put in at one of the lower
levels, by which stuff can be hauled from an extra
depth of 200 feet, and put on railway waggons in
the tunnel. Of hardly less advantage to the Rio

Tinto than the enormous abundance of its ore is
this facility of mining. Any known system of
working can be applied to it, and two or three may
be carried on abreast. Ultimately the north lode
is likely to be attacked both from above and below,
and the great force which can be turned on to it at
various points will soon bring to light whatever
may be in it. Mr Rich, cautious man as he is,
does not conceal that he entertains great hopes of
it. In one important respect it has the advantage
of the main lode ; the ironstone in the over-burden
is exceptionally rich, ranging up to 40 or 50 per
cent. Though it cannot be utilised at present,
it is not being thrown away ; but a great stack of
it is being formed near by, where one day it may
become a valuable " reserve." How to utilise the
48 per cent of iron contained in the Tinto ore is a
problem never lost sight of by the management,
though the prospect of its solution still seems
rather remote.

Returning to our North London analogy, several
characteristic features of Rio Tinto have yet to be
located. The calcining floors lie to the south-
east of the " open cast," and might, in relation to
the Mother Redcap, be a slice of St Pancras—a
very big slice, however, for they now extend over
many acres. The principal range of them lies in
a broad hollow on the side of a hill, and there are
outlying groups beyond. On the next terrace
below come the precipitating tanks, which are
also spreading out into acres, and filling up every

corner of available space. Lower still are the spoil, or rather wash heaps, consisting of the poorest ore, which will not bear the expense of any other treatment than filtering the copper out of it by running water. From time to time these heaps have spread out until the farthest of them is now as distant from the centre of the mine as Smithfield from the Mother Redcap. Recently, a new *terrero*, or wash ground, has been started in a large valley two or three miles down, which looks as if it would soon be filled up. The old heaps are being moved to it at the rate of a million tons of stuff a-year, and laid out in thinner layers, which accelerates oxidisation. The washing here has given so greatly improved results that the whole of the old heaps will be brought down. There is already enough to yield 4500 tons a-year of copper, which, with 4000 tons from the old heaps, assures the company of £340,000 per annum, even if not a ton of ore were to come out of the mine.

A MOORISH VILLAGE.

TOWNS are pretty much alike all the world over. Even in Spain they are fast losing their historical idiosyncrasies. You can have Bass, or Guinness, or Pilsener at the remotest corner of the Peninsula. Very probably the waiter who draws it for you tries to remind you of "home, sweet home" while you drink it, by observing that his brother Antonio is at Gatti's, or that he himself is from Gibraltar. Whether it be Gatti's or Gibraltar, he takes it out of you in his change. To see provincial Spain— real Spain—you must get far away from the reach of Guinness, or Bass, or Pilsener. Plunge into the Sierra Morena and explore some of its hidden valleys, where from time immemorial they have had no earthly thought save to grow olives, figs, and chestnuts ; or drop off at a wayside station in the great plain round Albacete. In either case you will stumble on very characteristic Spanish villages, where the old national life flows on slowly from generation to generation, where the Moorish tower of the village church is still the dominant object in the prospect, where girls gossip at the fountain in the *plaza* as girls have done for centuries, where the *posada* or village inn still keeps open its wide, hospitable, well-shaded door, where the windmills flap their wings as sleepily in the summer breeze as when they unconsciously challenged Don Quixote to mortal combat, and where the everlasting donkey trots along the dusty road as philosophically as when Sancho Panza favoured him with his confidential views on things in general and knight-errantry in particular.

Such a gem of an unadulterated Old World village is Chinchilla, on the railway from Albacete to Valencia. I claim very little credit for having discovered it. To confess the truth, it was done under compulsion and by stress of accident. In travelling from Madrid to Valencia I had made allowance for four changes of carriage, but there was a fifth that had been overlooked. Only at the last moment I escaped being taken unwittingly to Carthagena. Meanwhile the Valencia part of the train had gone on, and there were seventeen or eighteen hours to kill in waiting for the next. The first half-hour was excitingly, if not agreeably, spent in receiving the condolences and explanations of the railway officials who were not to blame, but were sorry all the same. Then I had a general survey of the landscape from the outside of the railway station. It was a rolling country with great stretches of flat land, broken by low hills, mostly isolated, but now and then extending into a short range.

Standing out from everything else, and arresting the eye at once, was a scarped hill, crowned by a crumbling old fortress. It was both striking and picturesque, its history being evidently as peculiar as its situation. It formed the high end of a ridge which, after rising gradually for twenty or thirty miles, had broken off short. The bold front it presented to the open plain had been originally steep and rugged, but the builders of the old fortress, whoever they were, had greatly modified its natural roughness. Its scarped sides had been cut into terraces, and the broken ground had been neatly sloped down. Narrow paths climbed from terrace to terrace up to the moat of the old fortress, and every terrace was crowded with houses. Mud cabins, houses, a couple of churches, a hospital, a theatre, and two or three public buildings of fair size, had been fitted into the scraps of building-space on the sides of the hill. Some were one shape and some another. Triangles and half-circles were very common, but full squares were rare.

"Admired confusion" had been carried to great lengths in Chinchilla. No two buildings looked in the same direction, or had the slightest relation to each other in size or shape. Here and there a brick hut seemed to be perched on the top of a house, while further on there would be a house looking as if it had grown out of the

huts below it. This ingenious result was achieved
by using the shelving rock for the back wall of
one building and the foundation of the next one
higher up. The chimneys were as lawless and
irregular as the houses themselves. They seemed
to be sometimes above and sometimes below you.
Where they did not threaten to tumble down on
you, you were in danger of tumbling into them.
They popped out of the ground at your feet; and
when you were on the point of jumping over a
ledge into the street below, you might discover
a red-tiled roof which you had very nearly gone
plump through, to the astonishment and alarm of
the owners.

In Chinchilla, and doubtless in many similar
villages in Spain, the chimney-exploring expedition of Asmodeus would be no strain whatever on
the imagination. Instead of there being anything
supernatural about it, or even fanciful, it would be
read as a familiar incident of everyday life. Not
only can you look down these funny chimneys of
Chinchilla, but you may sit on them if you like.
Many of them are not more than four or five feet
from the ground, and they finish with a broad top,
as if meant to be used for a look-out. In shape
they are like old-fashioned smelting-furnaces on
a small scale, and there is often more room in
them than in the cabins they ventilate. The latter are generally single apartments, the whole of
which can be seen from the outside. An iron
bedstead opposite the door, two or three straw-

bottomed chairs, a few cooking utensils hung on
the wall, and the inevitable water-jug, complete
their furniture. The floor is brick-paved or simply earth, and the walls are whitewashed outside
as well as in. Spain is the greatest country in
Europe for whitewash, and must use five times the
average quantity we do in England. Every two
months is an ordinary dose, but never less than
three or four times a-year.

Spanish villagers are much less liberal of sunlight than of whitewash. The smaller cabins have
no window to speak of, only a slit or a round hole
in the wall. The door, however, standing open as
it generally does, serves also for a window; but in
summer a heavy mat is hung up before it by all
who can afford the luxury. In larger houses there
is one principal window with a double sash opening lengthways. Decoratively, it is treated in a
variety of styles. A wooden railing may be put
across it, or the owner may be able to go to the
expense of iron bars, or his means may reach to
a balcony. Occasionally the light and graceful
double arch of the Moors may be found surviving in very old houses. It is the most beautiful
decoration of all. Secondary windows are mere
openings, square or round according to taste, but
seldom large enough to put the head out of.

In these semi-Moorish villages, houses differ
from each other mainly in size. They run on
the same lines, and the well-off man has merely
a little more elbow-room at home than the poor

man. Instead of a single cabin he has a series of them opening one out of the other. Less frequently there is a second floor, and rarely a courtyard. That distinction is most likely limited to the *posada* and the headquarters of the *Gobernio*. A village *posada* is a charming old place. First, there is the wide, ever-open door, inviting both mules and muleteers to enter. From it a broad causeway, paved with small stones, leads to the stables and the court behind. To the right or left opens from it the one public-room of the house, where eating, smoking, drinking, and washing have to be done. The washing arrangements are simplicity itself. In a niche in the wall the big water-jugs and a small basin are always ready. Latterly, a new fashion has come in of providing a few coarse towels. Two or three rooms off the large one are reserved for special guests; while the gay muleteer prefers to sleep as of old on the stone benches standing along the walls. The *posada*, so far as I have seen it, is no longer a thriving institution. The railways are killing it along with so much else of picturesque old Spain.

BEAUTIFUL BARCELONA.

ONE cannot go to Rome without seeing the Pope, or at all events dreaming that he has done so. If every other expedient should fail, the indefatigable Special can sup on lobster-salad, and in his visions of the night all the mysteries of the Vatican will be unfolded to him. The most secret and confidential thoughts of the Holy Father will be at his service for an interview which is to make crowned heads tremble and Imperial Chancellors feel jealous. So neither can a man be said to have seen Spain who has not been to Barcelona. But let him not begin at Barcelona. It is where he should rather finish if he wants an appropriate climax to the strange and novel impressions that will have been accumulating on him during his tour. At first I intended to go by Marseilles and Barcelona, and to return by the Pyrenees; but a friend who knows Spain well, and who also understands foreign travelling as an art, persuaded me to reverse the programme—to enter by the Pyrenees and leave by Barcelona. It was good advice, worthy of being passed on, which I do accordingly. By all means begin at the Pyrenees and finish at the Mediterranean. The arrangement has many advantages. The interest rises on an ascending scale, the scenery improves, and so does the economic condition of the people.

In Castile the Spaniard remains, as a rule, poor and primitive. Many centres of foreign enterprise, like Bilbao and Santander, have broken out round about him without shaking him much out of his old rut. Toward the south he wakes up, and has some faint notion of making a living for himself instead of expecting it from the Government. When we get round to Andalusia a surviving spirit of the Moors is traceable, and they are the only hard workers who ever were in Spain. Up through the orange-groves of Seville and the vine-yards of Valencia and Tarragona evidences of prosperity increase. Neither the Moselle Thal nor the best part of Burgundy would come out very well in competition with the vine-clad slopes which Spain presents to the Mediterranean. After such a panorama of beauties, a day or two in Barcelona is like passing out of a fairy land into a fairy city. The orange-groves disappear, to be succeeded by beautiful streets glowing overhead with colour, and below steeped in the grateful shadow of palm - trees. Before the olive - woods and the orchards are forgotten, a busy city full of shipping and commerce springs up in their place. A few

miles of a railway performs a marvellous transformation. It fires the sleepy, mooning Spaniard
of the interior with the adventurous spirit of the
north. He becomes a man of another race and
another character.

Barcelona is the essence and symbol of modern
Spain. Its people claim the special patronage of
Christopher Columbus. They have erected a noble
monument to him on the finest site their city
afforded — at the foot of their main street, the
Ramblas, and looking across the bay, which they
have made one of the busiest as well as one of
the prettiest harbours on the Mediterranean. It
is a magnificent work, after the style of our
Nelson column in Trafalgar Square, but, I believe,
higher, the total height from the ground to the
capital on which Columbus stands being over 160
feet. The figure which surmounts it is not only
colossal in size, but the attitude is striking —
Columbus pointing to the West—and the pose is
both forcible and dignified. The base is elabo-
rately ornamented with allegorical figures, partly
in bronze, partly in stone. They are, as a rule,
finely executed, and not a flaw or a commonplace
feature can be detected in the entire structure. It
is heroic throughout, and one could wish that all
our own public monuments were half so successful
in rising to the occasion. But what a contrast
between this proud column rearing its head in
the cloudless sky, and that poor, neglected little
monastery at the Rabida, where the living mem-

ory of Columbus and his expedition is truly en-
shrined !

Columbus promises to be a lucky patron for
Barcelona. Both the city and port are growing at
an unexampled rate, and mainly on the American
trade, of which he was the pioneer. It always was
the great Mediterranean *entrepôt* of Spain, and the
chief outlet for the fat harvests of Catalonia, but
of late it has spread its sails much wider. Its
transatlantic services are extending year by year,
and they now include South American as well as
northern ports. The principal line has weekly
steamers from Barcelona, calling at outports all
the way round to Santander and Bilbao. The
whole of Spain is thus served by native steam
lines across the Atlantic, and interest in America
is gradually growing. Till recently emigration
was an unknown idea to the Spanish peasant,
and for the middle-class Spaniard it meant only
official exile to Cuba. Now large numbers are
going forth to seek their fortunes across the sea.
They are erratic in their choice of new homes,
very few of them going to Mexico, which would
suit them best ; but every steamer for New York
has a full steerage, and such crowds are going
to the River Plate that very soon they will be
jostling the Italians there.

The details whereof may all be found in those
instructive, if rather promiscuous, publications of
the Foreign Office, the consular reports. It was
not strictly necessary to mention this, but I had

an ulterior object in doing so. It gives one an opportunity of fishing up an interesting reminiscence of the consular office at Barcelona — that twenty years ago it was filled by James Hannay. He did his fair share of consular reporting, doubtless, and if his statistics were not of the fullest, or arranged in the best possible order, there would be some neat English to hold them together. It may even be that the industrious gleaner might pick up one or two passable jokes among them. What induced Dizzy, I wonder, to select the Spanish coast as a Patmos for superannuated editors of the ' Edinburgh Courant'? James Mure, one of Hannay's successors, was consigned to the Balearic Islands—not far from Barcelona, but far enough to be a very different place. Dizzy died before the ' Courant,' or he might have repeated his Spanish joke on the last of the editorial unicorns of St Giles, who are supposed to have begun with Daniel Defoe. There might have been worse fates, too, than a consulship in beautiful Barcelona.

Were I a Madrileno I should feel jealous of Barcelona. Depend on it there is to be trouble between those two cities one day. It is another case of Edinburgh and Glasgow, or of Washington and New York. Madrid is the political capital, but Barcelona makes very small account of politics. It takes them as medicine now and then, and prefers them hot, but even then they are only a diversion. When Barcelona was younger, revolutioneering used to be a fashion among the working men. There was even a slight flurry among them the other day by way of expressing indignation at the muddle the Cortes has got into. It seldom does much harm, however, or becomes very formidable ; and as Barcelona increases in prosperity its blood seems to cool. The men I see about the docks at mid-day chatting and laughing over their dinner of bread and sardines or plain bread and cheese, do not look very bloodthirsty. They may have pikes and Phrygian caps concealed under their mattresses at home which they mean to bring out some fine morning, but the bread and sardines are the principal objects of their attention just now. It will be a strange madness indeed which ever prompts them to raise a hand against their own beautiful city—the pearl of the Western Mediterranean.

THE DESTINY OF SPAIN.

WHAT is going to happen to Spain is from every point of view an interesting and important question. The country is now in that half-and-half condition which admits of the most contradictory conclusions. If a man wished to prove that Spain was going to ruin financially and politically, he would not have far to go for plausible arguments. On the other hand, there is an equal abundance of proof that Spain is naturally one of the richest countries in the world, and if well handled might soon become one of the most prosperous. It is a glaring example of that most difficult of all economic problems—the nation which should get on but does not. It is more hopeless than a young country which has its career still to make. Spain has been made already more than once, but has always contrived to un-make itself again. It was one of the most flourishing provinces of Rome, but the moment the Romans left it it fell to pieces. Its so-called conquest by the Moors was the best thing that could have happened to it at the time. Instead of an invasion it should be called a regeneration, for it shed the light of science and literature over the southern half of the Peninsula when all the rest of Europe was plunged in monkish darkness.

Justice has yet to be done to that miracle of premature civilisation, the kingdom of Granada, which in the material arts anticipated our own century, and achieved engineering enterprises that would be hard to beat at the present day. The strip of coast-line cultivated by the Moors is still the most fertile part of Spain. In its day it was the best tilled district in Europe, and even yet it has not wholly lost that proud distinction. When the Moors were driven out their literature and their art departed with them, and for the second time Spain relapsed into the indolent barbarism which comes so naturally to her when left to her own devices. After several centuries of twilight, foreign hands again laid hold of her and raised her out of the dust. A Genoese mariner, Columbus, opened to her the gateways of the New World, and enabled her to enrich herself out of the inexhaustible treasure-houses of Mexico and Peru. Under Charles V. her destiny became allied with that of the Holy Roman Empire, and from a hornet's nest of quarrelsome provinces she rose to the supreme dignity of the leadership of Europe.

This third resurrection, glorious as it seemed, and powerful beyond reach of rivalry or mishap, passed away like a dream. A third time the

country of the Cid was humbled in the dust, and
the sceptre of Charles V. descended by degrees to
the nerveless hands of Ferdinand VI., while the
Cortes, which had made laws for the world, became
a forum for the rhetorical performances of Señor
Castelar.   Spain has been indeed unfortunate.
She has seen more ups and downs than any other
State in Christendom, and still her destiny is far
from being fulfilled.   The Spaniard is not played
out yet, and even the present generation may see
her in some respects as great a Spain as she has
ever been before.   She has much leeway to make
up, and more than one indispensable factor of
success appears to be still wanting to her.   Till
lately her industry and commerce have been on
the decline, but there is now reason to hope that
they have touched bottom.   This season her staple
crops have been better than for several years back,
and higher prices are being obtained for them.
The heavy taxation which weighs her down does
not yet admit of any relief, but the financial mis-
rule which causes it has reached a crisis, which
leaves no alternative but thorough reform or a
catastrophe.   Though the balance trembles, the
chances are slightly in favour of the happier issue.
The national finances are so terribly out of joint
that they cannot much longer be trifled with.   The
setting of them right has become not merely
urgent but imperative, and if Spanish politicians
wish to be thought anything better than mere

fiddling Neros, they will address themselves earnestly and patriotically to this subject in the present session of the Cortes.

The hour has struck for great events at Madrid, but the man is not yet there. A Spanish Cavour would find a task and an arena to satisfy his highest ambition. Let us hope that in due time he will present himself, and that his countrymen will recognise him when he comes: As yet no public man stands so decidedly head and shoulders above the political crowd as to be universally accepted as the saviour of the country. Party leaders there are in abundance, and able ones too, of their kind; but national leaders none. Señor Canovas has many of the personal qualifications for a heroic *rôle;* but all his life he has been too keen a party man to be able now to fire the dormant mine of patriotic enthusiasm. This is not the least of Spain's many misfortunes—subdivided leadership. Other States have known how to snatch salvation from supreme moments of national peril; but her perils seldom bring good out of evil. Her revolution of 1868 overwhelmed her with orators and jobbers, who between them made the meanest kind of a Government that even a brand-new republic was ever blessed with. While the one was tickling her ear with fine phrases, the other picked her pockets. Her civil wars produced but one passable general and statesman, Marshal Prim, and all her subsequent troubles have only kicked up the usual sort of parliamentary sawdust. The one strong sentiment of national unity which now prevails in Spain has been inspired by a woman and a foreigner. It is the chivalrous respect which Spaniards of all ranks and parties pay to the noble mother of their young king. The pure, womanly instincts of Queen Christina, and her self-sacrificing devotion to her adopted country, have drawn a charmed circle round the throne, turning into strength what seemed to be a fatal weakness.

If any political leader—Canovas or Sagasta for choice—could attract to himself such universal loyalty as the Queen Regent enjoys, and if he set himself vigorously to making the best use of it for the national benefit, miracles might soon be seen again in Spain. Why should it be impossible, or even difficult, for the Spaniards to accomplish what their own offspring in Mexico are doing so unexpectedly well? Ten, or even five years ago, the prospect of what Mexico is to-day would have been scoffed at as a Quixotic dream. She started at a great disadvantage as compared with Spain. Distance from Europe, ignorance of her capabilities, prejudice against her political record, the worst kind of financial credit, and the merest rudiments of industrial organisation, were all against her; but at the touch of a bold, intelligent brain they disappeared as if by magic. The cloud which hangs over Spain, concealing its unrivalled physical resources, would be quite as easily dispelled if a statesman, trusted of the whole nation, had a free hand to turn on it the sunlight of honest, capable administration. With all her faults, and in spite of her checkered past, Spain has still a great future to achieve.

THE most difficult lesson for the financial administrators of a country like Spain to learn, is the
supreme value of national credit. If they have
not been taught to look beyond the walls of the
Treasury, and to see that credit is a delicate network enveloping the whole nation, and affecting
its private as well as its public interests, they will
not be able to realise how important are the con-
sequences of any change in it, either for the better
or the worse. The Spaniards, as a people, have
not yet reached this high level of financial intelligence ; at all events, some of their representative
politicians talk as if they had not done so. In the
worst of their budgetary difficulties there has been
no proposal, or even suggestion, of direct repudiation ; but schemes for taxing coupons, which are
repudiation in disguise, are started often enough.
A not inconsiderable party in the Congress advo-
cates them on every occasion, and has done so
again during the past session. Such men, appa-

rently, cannot be made to see that a degradation of public credit would drag down all kinds of private credit along with it. Unfortunately for the practical effect of this argument, Spaniards have, as yet, made very little use of foreign capital compared with what they might do if they fully appreciated the opportunities they have of using it profitably. The non-saving class of them is very large, and easily contented, while the saving class is small and unenterprising. What little it has to invest it puts either in land or in Government securities.

Mortgages and the Four per cents, External or Internal, are the only investments known to the money - making Spaniard. Industrial enterprise he has next to none. He would not put his own money into the most promising of new industries, and why should he borrow from abroad for that purpose? So he reasons; and it may take some time to raise him out of his narrow view. With very little feeling of the need, much less of the value, of foreign capital, he cares very little whether Spanish Fours stand in London at 76 or at 72. In certain circumstances he rather welcomes a fall in price, for he may wish to come in as a buyer. To do them justice, intelligent Spaniards themselves believe in their own bonds, and of late years they are becoming an important element in sustaining the market for them. In the bear campaigns of 1886 and 1887 it was Madrid that defeated the bears, and not, as was supposed, the

I

"high finance" of Paris.   High finance can do
a great deal when it is swimming with the tide,
and has most of the facts in its favour ; but it
never of itself put up Spanish Four per cents to
76 in the teeth of a series of budgets showing
deficits of several millions sterling a-year.   These
would have broken the back of the bull syndicates,
as the Copper Ring smashed itself against facts
which were too strong for it.   They would long
ere now have reduced Spanish finance to as evil
a plight as Turkish, but for one essential difference
in the two cases.

The Turks never buy their own Government
stocks, or take any interest whatever in them.   To
a smaller extent the same may be said of the
Greeks in Greece.   Greek and Turkish securities
are consequently wanting in the strongest safeguard there can be for a national stock—the par-
ticipation in it of the people themselves.   Spanish
stocks, however, have that advantage to an increasing extent every year.   It has been estimated
lately that one-third of the exterior debt is now
held in the country, mainly as the result of pur-
chases made during the speculative collapse of
last year, and still more in that of 1887.   The
Bank of Spain always has been a large holder—
in truth, that was one of the chief, though un-
avowed, objects of its creation.   But its policy in
so doing is by no means unquestionable.   While
no harm, but only unmixed good, can come from
the holdings of Spanish bonds by the Spanish

people themselves, there is grave risk in the
national bank having a large portion of its capital
locked up in them. There can neither be sound
banking nor sound public finance while the two
are so closely mixed up together.

From a market point of view, it matters little
whether the domestic holding of Spanish bonds
be in the hands of a single institution or of several
thousand private investors; but the ultimate effect
on the bonds themselves may, in the two cases,
be very different. In the one it can only be a
conservative and sustaining influence; but in the
other it may involve greater risk than any foreign
holding, however speculative. Broadly speaking,
it may be affirmed that the Government stocks held
by the Bank of Spain are a danger both to it and
to them, while the private holdings in the country
are a sheet-anchor to them. *Prima facie* it says
a great deal for the ultimate safety of Spanish
bonds that the people themselves set the example
of believing in them. So it would be, in fact, if
the people understood the causes which keep their
bonds so low, and had the courage to apply the
only remedy. But as yet that would be rather too
much to expect of them. If they were sufficiently
practical in their business instincts to see that
budgets which never balance must one day come
to a violent end, they would insist on having them
reformed forthwith.

But no one seems to have that interest pure and
simple. Either they are mere tax-payers and do

not trouble themselves much whether the budget balances or not, or, if they be also bondholders, they have counteracting motives. They may have sons or brothers or cousins planted on the public service, besides others waiting to be planted at the first opportunity. A very impecunious Government has its special weaknesses to fight against. In Austria and Italy it is bloated armaments; in the British colonies it is public works, or "developing the resources of the country," as they call it; in Spain it is the civil service. The army, though large—about 300,000 men—cannot at the present international juncture be called either excessive or extravagant in its cost. In public works the Spanish Government is certainly not prodigal. It launches fine schemes enough, but generally they are to be carried out at somebody else's expense. If they be railways, they are conceded to one of the many syndicates which are continually hanging round in Madrid open-mouthed waiting for them; if they be roads, the provincial authorities have to take them in charge, and raise most of the money for them.

Spain is thus but poorly supplied with the stock pretexts of borrowing States. It cannot plead that its inability to live within its income springs from exceptional causes, or from burdening the present generation for the benefit of its successors. Its loans are not made, as a rule, for the improvement of the national estate, but merely to keep the administration going. That is the most sin-

ister feature in the Spanish deficits. They are
caused by the Government itself and its hordes of
employés. The Minister of Finance, who had a
free hand to do what he liked with the civil service, could, in a year or two, easily balance the
budget, or bring it at least near that point. The
Spanish Treasury, in short, is eaten up by officials,
precisely as Turkey is, but with the essential difference that in Turkey the officials, if they be too
numerous, do not get paid, while in Spain they are
all paid regularly. When once hoisted on Uncle
Sam's shoulders they are right for life. If they
have not been near their office all the month, their
salaries will be waiting for them all the same on
the first day of the following month. It is wonderful how busy and cheerful the public offices are
on pay-day compared with any other. This is the
primary cause of Spanish impecuniosity, though
there are many others allied with it. The problem is, consequently, both an easy and a difficult
one. Foreign capitalists, however powerful and
well-disposed, cannot lay hold of the Spanish
public service and cut it down to moderate pro-
portions; neither can Spanish ministers, unless
they have made up their minds to be the first
victims on the altar of retrenchment. But it will
have to be done one day, and possibly that day
is not far off.

SPAIN would be an easy country to govern if it did not cost money. Most other difficulties can be wrestled with, or dodged, or got round somehow, but a budget which will not balance cannot be trifled with. The yawning deficit it shows may be bridged over for a time, but it comes back again, like the perturbed and perturbing spirit of the royal Dane. When a deficit becomes normal, then it is a very uncomfortable complaint indeed. A Ministry cannot have anything on its mind more perplexing, not to say distressing. It may by long practice acquire callousness to financial criticism ; but creditors are creditors all the world over, and the most forbearing of them may at last lose patience. On the other hand, impecunious Ministers of Finance are not left wholly without hope and consolation. The worst pickle they can be in may be capped by something worse in past history.

Just now the Spanish Chancellor of the Ex-

chequer is regarded with universal interest and
sympathy because of the very tight corner in
which he finds himself. He is carrying by the
skin of his teeth a floating debt of eight or nine
millions sterling, the result of deficits inherited
from his predecessors. Till lately his revenue was
running behind at an alarming rate, and in the
fiscal year ended in June last, it exhibited a decline of over two millions sterling as compared
with 1887-88. Such a shrinkage might well de-
range any budget, and to a Spanish budget it is
fatal. Señor Gonzalez doubtless did his best
to curtail expenditure, and the provisional accounts show that he had some success, but
until finally adjusted they cannot be much relied
on. Evidently a large amount of special expenditure has been postponed. The budget, as
passed, exhibited a gross expenditure of fully
700 million pesetas, but up to the 30th June
only 689 millions had come into account. If we
were to believe the preliminary statement of the
Treasury, the year 1888-89 would have realised a
surplus—quite too good a thing to be true in the
present plight of Spanish finance. The actual
receipts are stated at 695 million pesetas, and the
expenditure at 689 millions. But the budget estimates were 919 millions and 1004 millions respectively; therefore a good deal has yet to be brought
to book on either side. When the accounts for
1888-89 are closed, the inevitable deficit will be
there as usual, and whether it be ten or twenty

million pesetas more or less is of secondary consequence.

The Finance Minister has now three critical questions to face—the nine millions sterling of accumulated deficits, the eighteen millions sterling of Government securities which the Bank of Spain is jammed up with, and the fact that the bank has reached the full legal limit of its note issue. Its existing capital is 150 million pesetas, and it is authorised to issue notes to five times that amount, which would make 750 million pesetas. During the past half-year its circulation has hovered within a million or two of the maximum, and the cause of that is as peculiar as the thing itself. The trade of the country has not required any additional supply of currency, or at least only a small portion of what has been created. A year or two ago it had enough with 400 or 500 million pesetas, and it has not visibly expanded since. But the necessities of the Treasury have expanded, and they have had to be satisfied with whatever could be got—if not gold, then paper. The 200 million pesetas of accumulated deficits, and the 250 millions of additional paper money, have an obvious connection with each other. If the Treasury debt to the bank could be liquidated, they might be wiped out together. A new loan of ten millions sterling or thereabouts would be a great relief to the Government; ere long it may become an imperative necessity. Then the old, old question would have to be threshed out all over again, whether or not it is safe to lend more money to Spain?

That is a question which many financial authorities would answer off-hand with a decided negative. Others may charitably admit a doubt, or a half-doubt, of which Spain should have the benefit. In attempting to resolve so knotty a point, which admits of so much being said on both sides, one reverts almost unconsciously to examples of even worse budgets than those of Spain which have come out all right in the long-run. Bad as the financial situation is in Madrid, it has still some distance to go before it reaches the depths of despair in which the Austrian Treasury floundered for a quarter of a century. Its deficits were more formidable, more continuous, and apparently more hopeless than the Spanish, and yet the Austrian budget has reached equilibrium. Italy offers another encouraging precedent. For years after its national unity had been won at the point of the sword, it was in danger of being lost again through national insolvency. But Italy, too, weathered the storm, and why may not Spain? All that is needed is for Spanish statesmen to imitate the resolution and self-sacrifice exhibited at Vienna and Rome. By cutting down expenses with one hand and developing revenue with the other, the two ends can be made to meet within a reasonably short time.

The bare figures of a budget may be a superficial and misleading test of the financial ability

of a State like Spain. Underlying them are much
more important elements in the calculation—the
tax-bearing strength of the community, the character of the public administration, the progress or
otherwise of national wealth, and a host of kindred
data. Whether or not Spain could bear heavier
taxation without a strain is a question for domestic,
rather than for foreign criticism. But it may be
allowable to apply one or two rough standards of
comparison. Spain has a home population of
about seventeen millions, and its public revenue
averages in normal years thirty millions sterling.
If the whole amount were derived from taxes it
would represent 35s. per head, but only three-fifths
of it is, properly speaking, fiscal. The other two-
fifths are the produce of State monopolies, State
property, and Treasury receipts of various kinds.
For these 14s. per head may be deducted from the
gross revenue, and the balance of 21s. per head is
the true standard of Spanish taxation. No one
will call it an oppressive amount even for a poor
country. Frenchmen have three times as heavy a
bill to pay to their rulers ; and even the Belgians,
well governed as they are, have almost double the
Spanish rate of taxation to bear.

If any dire necessity arose calling for patriotic
sacrifices, the Spanish taxpayer could contribute
more to the State, and yet not be severely bur-
dened in comparison with similar communities
elsewhere. But the easier remedy may be tried
beforehand. There can be little doubt but that

existing taxes would yield more to the Treasury
if more viligantly collected. The falling off in
the past two years has been set down to bad
times, but the fiscal service itself may have had
some share of responsibility. The trade returns
and other official records do not indicate that
Spain has been retrograding at such a rate as
the revenue receipts suggest. Two millions loss
on a total of thirty millions sterling a-year would
be equal to seven per cent. Spanish industry has
not shrunk seven per cent, or even one per cent.
It has been improving all the time, though, perhaps, at a slower rate than in the prosperous years
1886 and 1887. In the first six months of the
current year (1889) the imports were higher by
seven million pesetas, and the exports by forty-six
million pesetas ; but, strange to say, the Customs
duties showed a reduction of fifteen million pesetas.
Revenue and trade have not been going hand in
hand as they ought to do, and the taxpayers are
evidently faring better than the Treasury. An
explanation is needed of this paradox.

HER INDUSTRIAL CAPABILITIES.

SPANISH statistics take a long time to mature, but when fully matured they are both elaborate and valuable. As regards population, they are still operating on the census of 1877, according to which there were 16,634,000 souls on the Peninsula and the adjacent islands. The Antilles, including Cuba and Porto Rico, had an additional 2¼ millions, and the Philippines 5½ millions. Under the Spanish Crown there are consequently 24½ millions of subjects distributed over some of the richest portions of the globe. *Prima facie* there should be no insuperable obstacle to such a community paying its way, even without a perfect system of government. A first-class State has more than once been built up with smaller materials. The whole of South America, Brazil included, contains only a few millions more people than Spain and her colonies have. The next question is as to their productive value. For a test of that, we may take Spain's wealthy and energetic neighbour France, as to whose industry there can be no doubt. Somewhat less than 38 millions of Frenchmen export at the rate of 120 millions sterling per annum. In years of high prices, like 1876 and 1882, it has risen to over 140 millions sterling, but in bad times it has been as low as 123 millions sterling. The mean here adopted gives an average of nearly £3, 10s. per head. The 16,600,000 Spaniards produce for export about 30 millions sterling per annum. The total has been in some years 34 millions, and in others as low as under 20 millions sterling. At 30 millions it gives an average of £1, 15s. per head—exactly one-half of the French rate.

Here is one palpable cause of the difference in economic condition between these two nations— one on the north and the other on the south side of the Pyrenees. When Spanish exports approach the French level, Spain will be as prosperous a country as France, and possibly more so, for she has advantages which France does not enjoy, and is not likely to in our day. Exports are only a small part of the industrial range of a community. It may be estimated that domestic consumption represents three times as much more. France, on this basis, would produce and consume at home 390 millions sterling a-year against 130 millions exported, and her national industry would be worth altogether over 500 millions sterling a-year—obviously a very moderate estimate. At the same rate the home production and consumption of Spain would be 90 millions sterling a-year, which, added to 30 millions of exports, make a national industry of 120 millions sterling a-year. The figures need only to be stated in order to demonstrate what a wide margin there is for industrial development in Spain. Very probably the present generation will see Spanish exports trebled and home consumption increased on a still larger scale. That is going to be one factor in the solution of the financial dead-lock. It is almost bound to come whether other ameliorations happen or not. The worst Government which would be tolerated nowadays cannot long repress the growth of a nation so surrounded with opportunities as Spain is on all hands.

Reasons for being sanguine about the future of the Peninsula are not far to seek. They may be found by the dozen in the census tables, some of them very characteristic as well as interesting. The industrial status of a population is always significant, and in Spain particularly so. The following is the classification officially arrived at in the 1877 returns :—

	Per cent.
Commercial, ...	0.80
Transport, ...	0.95
Industrial, ...	1.26
Diverse occupations, ...	2.59
Liberal professions, ...	2.99
Officials, ...	4.06
Agriculturists, ...	29.87
Without profession, ...	57.48

The first three classes are amusing, and not less so is the last. Hardly one Spaniard in a hundred condescends to soil his ancient lineage by associating it with trade. They think it a shade less degrading, apparently, to whack mules or sport railway uniform, than to keep shop, though all three occupations put together make up a very puny total. Artisans number about one in eighty of these charming lotus-eaters ; and miscellaneous occupations are claimed by one in forty. Everything that the census-takers can, by any stretch of indulgence, call an industry, when collected and analysed, makes less than 6 per cent of the population, or, say, *one in seventeen*. When we turn to the genteel modes of life, the figures grow rapidly. Liberal professions absorb nearly 3 per cent, and officials *over 4 per cent*. Here, manifestly, is where the shoe pinches in Spain. One person in twenty-five prefers being kept by the State to keeping himself. He will be a clerk in the post-office, a tide-waiter, a baggage-searcher in the Custom-house — anything with a bit of gold lace and a salary to it, rather than forage for his own living. It is a bad choice, both for him and the country. Nine-tenths of the men who thus vegetate as officials, have brains enough and opportunities enough to treble their starvation incomes if they would only pocket their pride and throw a little more energy into the process of existence. The State, on its side, would be better served if it were rid of one-half of them.

Officialism is the curse of Spain, and the Hercules who can strangle that snake which, in ever-lengthening folds, coils itself round the Treasury, will be the first practical reformer in Spanish politics. His next exploit might be to annihilate the swarms of beggars who infest every public place in the Peninsula. They rank, I believe, as one of the learned professions, and in point of numbers they run the priests rather close. The agriculturist, who is the backbone of the country, must have a hard time with so many parasites hanging on to him. He forms less than a third of the population—29.87 per cent—and has to work for all. Farmers are one of the few classes of Spaniards who are better than their reputation. Report pictures them as lazy, fanciful, and erratic. They are, in fact, laborious, peaceable, and plodding. Whether toiling alone on their little farms, or working in groups at the mines or marble-quarries, they are, I am assured, satisfactory workers. At the Rio Tinto they have been employed side by side with Cornishmen, and better value for the money has been got out of them. In such establishments the use of native labour is increasing, and rising in quality at the same time. Responsible duties, such as engine-driving and ore-picking, are now intrusted to Spaniards which formerly were reserved for Englishmen or Germans.

The Spanish labourer is very little to blame for the slow progress of his country. He has, at the worst of times, done his share fairly well, and since he came under skilled leadership he has improved greatly. There is as good labour, both skilled and unskilled, to be got in most parts of Spain as anywhere else in Europe, not excepting England. There need be little fear on that score in undertaking any new enterprise in the Peninsula. The Spaniard is eminently teachable, and on piece-work he soon outgrows any tendency he may have to mooning around and counting his beads. From sunrise to sunset he can keep the hammer going, not fast but steadily. Half an hour for breakfast, two hours for dinner, five minutes for his cigarette at mid-day, and another five in the afternoon, are all the rest he needs in the longest summer day. He may lay off occasionally when he has a few pesetas to spend, but while at it he works regularly, and makes good wages. Labourers fit for heavy work like mining, quarrying, railroading, earn little if any less in Biscaya or Andalusia than in Lancashire or Yorkshire. Only of late has this great economic improvement set in, and its effects are yet in embryo; but they may soon be strong enough to help the Treasury out of its chronic deficits.

All the requisite elements of profitable industry exist in Spain; the only trouble is that they have not yet learned to co-operate effectively. Capital has been accumulating from generation to generation since it first began to flow in from the New World. Bone and sinew abound in

K

every Spanish village, and brain is running to seed among the educated classes for sheer lack of employment. Enterprises are to be had in boundless variety which should weld muscle and brain together in a co-partnery of success and progress. Spain is slowly awakening to the fact that the days of knight-errantry are over, and that a new age of prosaic hard work has set in. Though the last of the ancient nations to give up castles in the air for factories and foundries on solid earth, she may not have to lag much longer in the rear. Her resources are so vast, her commercial facilities so rare, and her national character in many respects so sound, that regeneration when it begins, will flash through the land like a flood of sunlight.

HER RAILWAYS.

NEXT to the Rio Tinto mines, which were the special object of my pilgrimage, the railways of the country have received chief attention: for two reasons,—first, that Spanish railway securities are practically unknown in our English stock market; and second, that the Peninsula offers now the best field in Europe for railway enterprise. Spain has reached the industrial stage at which further progress depends mainly on two conditions —both financial. One is the rehabilitation of the national credit, and the other the development of cheap and rapid transport. She is at the critical point when foreign capital may be of invaluable help, and the question of how to get it must be of vital importance. The foundation and mainspring of all finance in a borrowing country like Spain are the Government bonds. The national Treasury, as the chief borrower, sets the tune for all private borrowers. If Spanish Four per cents could be raised to par, the market price of railway securities, bank shares, and joint-stock investments would improve proportionately. The rate of interest on mortgages would decline with the yield of the State bonds, and the country all round would enjoy the benefits of comparatively cheap money. The farmer's crop would leave him a better balance for himself; the manufacturer would have a better home market and larger profits; the labourer would be in greater demand, and receive higher wages. The process by which foreign capital fertilises a poor country is as simple as the circulation of water or the production of steam. There is no dubiety or risk about it—no possibility of failure. It operates in all parts of the world just the same, irrespective of colour, language, or climate. Spain is waiting for the benefit of it, and there is abundance of capital ready to flow in as soon as the confidence of capitalists can be secured.

The primary condition of a free influx of money is faith in the national credit. That is passing now through a severe ordeal, and very pessimist views of it are entertained in many quarters; but the people who know it best are confident that it will come out all right. Let us, for the present, accept their authority, and proceed to the railway question. Spanish railways have many faults, which get noised abroad by every traveller; but they have also a few good and promising qualities, for which they get very scant credit. Like our own, they have grown up rather at haphazard, and seldom take the nearest line from point to point. Not even from Madrid can you go anywhere by a reasonably direct route. The original main lines meander from north to south and from east to west, in apparently the most gratuitous fashion. On the map they show great loops and bends, which might be cut out of them with much advantage to themselves and the traffic. How these arose is a rather intricate inquiry. Part of the cause, no doubt, was the mileage system of subsidy, which put a strong temptation in the way of contractors to make length for its own sake.

The Spanish Government has a curious method of subsidising railways. It pays a lump sum down, and not an annual contribution, as the South American republics do. The old contractors had, consequently, a direct inducement to run up the number of kilometres. The monetary advantage it gave them involved another of hardly less consequence. It enabled them to go round about in search of easy country, and of districts likely to yield the best traffic. The Northern of Spain had some excuse for dodging about among the passes of the Pyrenees; but after it had got out of them, it indulged in a gratuitous sweep to the westward. Burgos and Madrid are in almost the same longitude; but you cannot go from one to the other without making a five or six hours' detour to Medina, which is fully a hundred miles west of both. The only railway in Northern Spain which makes any approach to straightness is the one from Miranda to Bilbao, over which the late Mr Brassey lost so much money. It is a splendid piece of railway work, but very heavy. In order to get up the hill out of Bilbao it has to mount an incline as severe and much longer than that at the Glasgow Queen Street station; and this is but the first of a long series. The train, drawn by enormous engines, is continually running up hill or down, and when not on a stiff grade it is in a deep cutting or a long tunnel. It appears now that an easier and shorter route might have been got by running from Vittoria instead of Miranda, and a second line by that route is projected.

The farther inland we go the circumbendibus system becomes more remarkable, until we get right down to the south coast, where a notable example of a short-cut railway presents itself in the Zafra and Huelva. It is built on the new principle of going straight ahead, and combining the shortest distance with the best grades obtainable. That is expensive in the first instance, when you have a high mountain-range to cross, like the Sierra Morena; but it has compensations. The risk of competition is greatly reduced, whether from the irrepressible mule and donkey, or from new railways. Through business will naturally be drawn to the shortest, and, for passengers, most picturesque route. The wilder the region the better the chance of some great mineral discovery, which will create at a stroke as much traffic as the road can carry. Already the Zafra and Huelva has struck one *bonanza* of that kind. At Val de la Moussa, about twenty-three miles north of Huelva, a French company is opening up a pyrites-mine, which is the most remarkable deposit of that kind yet discovered. It forms a vast basin, like the "open cast" in Rio Tinto, and the pyrites is dry and perfectly pure—there is hardly a trace in it of copper or arsenic. Though losing in commercial value by the absence of these compounds, it is preferred by the sulphuric acid makers for its purity, and has consequently a free market. Until the railway came it could not be worked at a profit, but cheap transport has turned the scale in its favour. Hundreds of men are now at work in the mine, which looks like an infant Rio Tinto, and the freight put on the railway averages 800 tons a-day.

Other discoveries in the same neighbourhood— or, indeed, in any part of the Sierra—may happen any day, and the railway which has secured all this region to itself must soon have traffic enough to make up for the extra cost of its first construction. I have already referred to the marble-quarries higher up at Fuente Herridos, which are going to be another special feeder of the Zafra and Huelva. The probability is that it will, in course of time, be fringed with mines all the way through; and at its northern end it taps the rich granary of Estramadura, which hitherto has had no direct outlet to the coast. As an example of the new style of Spanish railway, the Zafra and Huelva will well repay future attention.

The older Spanish railways were gradually combined into three great systems, each of them controlled by a certain financial group. The Northern of Spain, starting from the frontier at Irun, owns the main line down to Madrid, and has covered the whole of the western provinces with a network of branches. San Sebastian, Bilbao, Santander, and all the Biscay ports down to Corunna, it has laid under tribute. To the eastward it is also throwing out feeders, like its cross-country line from Miranda to Saragossa; but its proper territory continues to be the northwest, embracing roughly all the old State of Castile. Its controlling power is the Pereire group in Paris, who dictate its policy and regulate the market in its securities. The second, or Rothschild system, starts from Madrid, and ramifies all over the south. It is known by the rather cumbrous name of Madrid, Saragossa, and Alicante, which, long as it is, covers only a small part of the network. "The Great Southern of Spain" would be a shorter, and, at the same time, more adequate designation. And even that would still not be strictly accurate, for one of the best parts of the company's property—the line from Madrid to Saragossa—has a north-easterly direction. With that important exception, the whole system is south of the capital.

A glance on the map at the Madrid, Saragossa,

and Alicante, will show that, as a railway network, it has grown fortuitously, without much planning. It is quite American in the freedom with which it sprawls over the country. Entering Spain from the Portuguese side, you strike it at Badajoz, and are glad to meet with it, for its carriages and its service generally are an obvious improvement on the Portuguese ; or, if you enter from the Mediterranean side, you will find it at Alicante ; or, once more, come in from the Atlantic on the extreme south, and it will pick you up at Huelva. From Badajoz on the west, Alicante on the east, and Huelva on the south, the Rothschild system commands all the through routes to Madrid. It may not be destined to enjoy its monopoly for ever, or, indeed, for many years more; but as it exists now, it is one of the great factors in Spanish railway policy.

A system much smaller in mileage than either of these, but powerful through having the richest traffic in the country at its mercy, is the Almansa, Valencia, and Tarragona. It starts from the Rothschild network at Almansa, and covers the whole paradise of the Peninsula—that broad belt of vineyards, orchards, olive and orange groves, which stretches along the Mediterranean coast from Alicante to Barcelona. In fertility and perfection of culture this is incomparable. The Lothians are an unkempt wilderness beside it. Every inch of ground is tilled, till neither clod nor weed is to be seen on it. Every tree and plant is a brilliant, healthy green, without a faded leaf or a scraggy branch anywhere. Water-courses are carried round all the fields, however small, and at pleasure the owner can turn them on wherever he . needs them. So valuable is space that the groves and vineyards come up close to the railway. They seem to grudge it room to pass, and from a carriage-window you may often touch an orange or an olive tree in shooting past. No other railway I have ever seen has got so thoroughly into the heart of the Garden of Eden as the Almansa, Valencia, and Tarragona. It could not avoid having a magnificent traffic ; and the long lines of trucks, either loading or unloading at each station, tell at once that it is doing well. It pays the best dividends of any Spanish railway, though they are no longer quite so good as they used to be, extensions and branches not yet developed having pulled down the average return on its capital.

On the skirts of these three chief systems hang a number of secondary railways, like the Zafra and Huelva ; the Andalusian lines which connect Granada, Malaga, and Cadiz with the Rothschild network at Cordoba ; the line from Barcelona to the French frontier, controlled, I believe, by the Paris, Lyons, and Mediterranean ; and a number of new ventures in the Biscay provinces. There is a strong tendency all over the country toward railway development. The Government and the

Cortes are both committed to a policy of assisting secondary lines in the poorer districts. Most of these will be feeders to the main lines, and might be best built by them; but all three of the great systems seem to have had as much extension of that kind as they care for at present. They painfully realise the bad effect it had a few years ago on their dividends and the market value of their securities. Having just begun to recover from that chill, they are not unnaturally disposed to let well alone as long as they can. But all the same, many branch lines are being projected, and will be made by somebody, for they are really wanted, and circumstances appear to be in their favour. Railway progress in Spain is, curiously enough, in a similar stage to what it has reached in India. The skeleton of main lines has been laid down, and the filling up of it with ribs and muscle has begun.

While most of the new railways in contemplation will simply be branches or feeders, one class of them aims at a more important function. They are intended to correct the original errors of the main lines in not taking the most direct routes, or securing the best possible grades. No two important towns in the country can be said to have the shortest connection open to them. There is nearly everywhere a great and growing need of what the Americans expressively term " cut-offs." A few have been made, and many more are pro-

jected. Some important ones have been authorised by the Cortes, and are in progress. Railway
building is, in fact, very active in Spain and
Portugal just now, though few of our English
railway contractors appear to be much alive to
the fact. To take only one district—Estramadura,—a short cut is to be made from Zafra across
to Badajoz, and another further north from Caceres
up to Salamanca. These, if they go through all
right, will not only benefit greatly the districts
they traverse, but will open up a new route from
south to north, avoiding altogether the detour
vià Madrid.

There is, of course, a conservative party who
object to new projects, and predict that they will
never pay. What will pay in Spain has never
yet been seriously tested. The French style of
management has prevailed from the beginning
on all the main lines, and though it has its good
qualities, it may not be the best suited to a
growing country. In an old and settled community like France, its lack of elasticity may
not be much felt; but it soon tells where traffic
does not exist, but has to be created. French
railway men are good organisers and excellent
accountants; perhaps no better system of statistics than theirs is to be found. They are not,
however, creative. They have too many hard-
and-fast rules, and are slow to see openings for
new business. It wrings their heart to reduce a

tariff, and the idea of giving special rates would seem to them contrary to liberty, equality, and fraternity. Seeing how primitive the traffic still is, one can hardly believe that these Franco-Spanish lines have been open now for over twenty years. All things considered, they are small for their age.

HER RAILWAY FINANCE.

THE warmest champion of Spain will have to admit that in some things she is not up to date. From the company promoter's point of view she is years behind the age. It is only of late that he has got his hand in at all, and even yet he has to limit his enterprise to the most legitimate kinds of business, such as railway building, banks, finance companies, &c. Electric lighting is the only novelty in joint-stock wares to which the Spaniard is at all partial. Taken altogether, the Peninsula is poorly supplied with joint-stock securities of native growth. The latest official statistics only come down to the end of 1884, when there were about 260 companies of various kinds registered. They are classified as under in the census report as

Concessionary Companies—
For railways,	.	.	46
For tramways,	.	.	22
For public works,	.	15	
		—	83

Brought forward,	. .	83
Banks and discount companies,	.	16
Water, .	. . .	12
Gas and electricity,	. . .	15
Agricultural,	. . . .	6
Insurance,	. . . .	11
Transport,	. . . .	17
Manufacturing, .	. . .	42
Industrial,	. . . .	56
		258

Railways form by far the most important category, and their statistics make a fairly respectable show both in mileage and expenditure, and also in earning power. At the end of 1884 there had been 8485 kilometres constructed, but it is characteristic of the country that a considerable portion was not in operation. The working length was 8140 kilometres, so that 345 kilometres was, for some reason or other, dormant. The aggregate capitalisation up to that date was 2367 million pesetas. The peseta may be taken roughly as a franc, and 2367 millions of them would be nearly 95 millions sterling. The 8485 kilometres being equal to 5090 miles, a total cost of 95 millions sterling would give the apparently large average of about £19,000 per mile. The actual money put into them had been much less, their capital having been issued on the French system of large discounts. The 763 million pesetas of share capital was placed probably at an average of 50 per cent—that is, 250 francs for the 500 franc share, and the 1603 million pesetas of obligations at 60 per cent, or 300 francs for 500 francs nominal. The actual cost per kilometre may be fairly estimated at £9000 to £10,000 per mile ; a very moderate rate, allowing for the heavy country which many of the lines have to traverse.

Most of the forty-six railways are short lines—a good many of them less than a hundred kilometres —but the inevitable process of consolidation is already at work among them. There are three leading systems, each of considerable magnitude, and worked with a fair degree of energy. Foremost in length and in amount of capital is the Rothschild system — Madrid, Saragossa, and Alicante. It measured, at the end of 1884, 2625 kilometres, and its capital account stood at 874 million pesetas—an average of 330,800 pesetas per kilometre—equal to £21,000 per English mile. Its gross receipts averaged 19,600 pesetas per kilometre = £1330 per mile per annum. The nearest parallel to it among our own railways would be the London and South-Western, which, on 870 miles, earns over three millions sterling a-year, just making an average of £3600 per mile, or nearly treble that of the Madrid, Saragossa, and Alicante. The latter has the advantage of low working expenses—43.83 per cent, which is almost 10 per cent below the London and South-Western proportion. The second longest system is the Northern of Spain —a network which extends in one direction from the Pyrenees to the Portuguese frontier, and in another from the Bay of Biscay to the Mediterranean. Its various sections make up an aggregate of 1852 kilometres, or 1110 English miles. Its capitalisation amounts to 626½ million pesetas, an average of nearly 340,000 pesetas per kilometre, or fully £22,000 per mile. But its earning power is correspondingly large ; one section of it having yielded as much as 36,000 pesetas per kilometre, while the poorest produced 22,500 pesetas. Its working expenses ranged from 37 up to 44¾ per cent of gross receipts. The actual cost varied from 9425 pesetas to 13,400 pesetas per kilometre, which we may average at 11,000 pesetas per kilometre, or £733 per English mile, as against £2000 per mile on the London and South-Western.

Of the main systems, the best paying is the Tarragona and Barcelona, which runs through the garden of Spain along the upper shores of the Mediterranean to the French frontier. Its length is under 350 kilometres, or 210 English miles, and it is capitalised at 136,758,000 pesetas, which gives an average of nearly 400,000 pesetas per kilometre, equal to £26,600 per mile. But it earns at the rate of over 40,000 pesetas per kilometre on an expenditure of 16,800 pesetas. In English currency that is £2660 per mile of gross receipts, and £1120 of working expenses. Closely connected with the Tarragona and Barcelona is another prosperous road, paying handsome dividends to its shareholders. The Almansa, Valencia, and Tarragona traverses the lower half of the great orange

growing region ; and being lightly capitalised—
only 82½ million pesetas per 407 kilometres, or
at the rate of 200,000 pesetas per kilometre—it
enjoys relatively high returns. Its gross receipts
average 25,000 pesetas per kilometre, against
11,500 pesetas for kilometre of working expenses.
Put in English, that comes to £1660 per mile of
gross receipts, and £766 per mile of working
expenses.

But the *bonanzas* of the Spanish railway system
are to be sought for among the short local lines
having a special traffic. The Triano, which is the
principal ore-carrying line at Bilbao, cost 658,000
pesetas per kilometre, or £44,000 per mile to
build, but it earns yearly 291,000 pesetas per
kilometre, fully £19,000 per mile. Two years and
a half of gross revenue covers the whole original
cost of construction. The working expenses are
only 44 per cent, and out of the remaining 56 per
cent it is not difficult to pay brilliant dividends.
The Triano is the Taff Vale of the Peninsula, and
some of our speculative railway contractors might
do worse than take a look round Bilbao in search
of openings for another Triano line. It has already an English rival in the Bilbao River and
Cantabrian, a short road of 21 kilometres, but the
great hematite field will stand much more railway
development. These Biscayan mountains in the
north, and the Sierra Morena in the south, offer
boundless scope to the railway builder as well as
to the mining engineer. It is in the odd corners

rather than in the main body of the Peninsula that traffic is to be created. The general railway business of Castile or Leon bears no comparison with that of Bilbao ; neither is that of the Andalusian system to be mentioned for a moment beside the huge volume of traffic passing over the Rio Tinto line. The former, which connects the South Mediterranean ports of Spain with Granada and Seville, has a length of 776 kilometres, and is capitalised at the rate of 120,000 pesetas per kilometre, or £8000 per mile. But it earns only 14,500 pesetas per kilometre gross, and 7800 pesetas net, equal to £960 and £510 per mile respectively. Its gross receipts are only 12 per cent of its capital cost, and the net little more than 6 per cent.

A favourable feature of the older Spanish railways is the comparative cheapness of their working ; but whether this be due to genuine economy or to high rates of freight, is not ascertainable with certainty. On the trunk lines the rate of working expenses is invariably under 50 per cent, and occasionally as low as 40 per cent. On the shorter and younger lines it is naturally higher. The Asturias Railway (Galicia and Leon) costs as much as 65 per cent to work. The new direct line from Madrid to Lisbon *viâ* Caceres, when it was first opened, earned only about £550 per mile per annum gross, and over 68 per cent of it was swallowed up by working expenses. One of the Andalusian lines (Alicante to Murcia) started also with a heavy working rate—about 88 per cent ; and a short line (Selgua to Barbostro) worked by the Northern of Spain, cost 3 per cent more than its earnings to keep it in operation. Such experience, however, is not unknown in England, and it is familiar enough in American railway finance.

Taken all round, Spanish railways appear to be carefully administered, and those of them which have had time to develop their resources, are making a fair return on their actual cost. Their results offer every encouragement to new enterprises of the same class. Many are being projected, and the Minister of Public Works at Madrid is beset by concession hunters from every part of Europe. The railway contractor and the railway financier have just now a keen scent for Spanish concessions.

THE END.

www.ingramcontent.com/pod-product-compliance
Lightning Source LLC
Chambersburg PA
CBHW020545270326
41927CB00006B/723